Friendship and Second Innocence

Friendship and Second Innocence

John Howard Griffin
and Tommy McKillop

Foreword by Benedict Vanier
Preface by Bill Wittman

NOVALIS

© 2008 Novalis, Saint Paul University, Ottawa, Canada

Cover and layout: Dominique Pelland, Francine Petitclerc
Cover Image: © Jupiter Images
Interior photographs: Bill Wittman, except where otherwise noted

Business Offices:

Novalis Publishing Inc.
10 Lower Spadina Avenue, Suite 400
Toronto, Ontario, Canada
M5V 2Z2

Novalis Publishing Inc.
4475 Frontenac Street
Montréal, Québec, Canada
H2H 2S2

Phone: 1-800-387-7164
Fax: 1-800-204-4140
E-mail: books@novalis.ca
www.novalis.ca

Library and Archives Canada Cataloguing in Publication

Griffin, John Howard, 1920-1980.
    Friendship and second innocence / John Howard Griffin and Tommy McKillop ; foreword by Benedict Vanier ; preface by Bill Wittman.

ISBN 978-2-89646-005-2

    1. Griffin, John Howard, 1920-1980–Correspondence. 2. McKillop, Tom, 1928- –Correspondence. 3. Friendship–Religious aspects–Catholic Church. I. McKillop, Tom, 1928- II. Title.

BX4651.3.G75 2008   282.092'2   C2008-901476-6

Printed in Canada.

All rights reserved. No part of this publication may be reproduced, stored in a retrieval system, or transmitted in any form, or by any means, electronic, mechanical, photocopying, recording, or otherwise, without the written permission of the publisher.

We acknowledge the financial support of the Government of Canada through the Book Publishing Industry Development Program (BPIDP) for our publishing activities.

5 4 3 2 1   12 11 10 09 08

*A man can have no greater love
than to lay down his life
for his friends.*

John 15:13

Dedication

For those who are searching for an inclusive friendship,
feel a struggle within,
yet in your deepest self
sense a mysterious call to second innocence in Jesus.

This is my gift
from Jesus

And to Jesus
And to all

Who might read
this book

What comes to my mind
and heart
are the graced
words of
Meister Eckhart:

"If the only prayer
you say in your entire life
is 'Thank You'
that would suffice."

–Tommy McKillop

Acknowledgments

Mrs. Joan Mellon, a devoted friend, a committed member of the Legion of Mary and a faithful member of St. John Chrysostom Parish, came as an alternative secretary to type the manuscript, as well as to put in order the whole text according to the context of the letters. For all her typing and careful work, I am profoundly grateful. Thanks also to her grandson, Francis Coral Mellon, who burned the original manuscript onto the CD.

Alan Fujiwara designed the original Youth Corps logo. An adapted version of this logo is featured in white in the background of the back cover of this book.

Mr. Bill Wittman generously and beautifully provided the photographs for the book.

Thanks also to Alf McCabe, who made such memorable paintings of the early participants in the Youth Corps events, including Dorothy Day and John Howard Griffin.

Over a period of years, Mario Zuniga, a devout supporter of the works of John Howard Griffin, expressed his support to me to complete the manuscript.

Robert Bonazzi, the second husband of John Howard's wife, Piedy, encouraged me to carry on *Second Innocence*. On July 20, 1996, Robert wrote,

"Keep working on that – and all this – in your prayers, contemplation, intellection."

Benedict Vanier, my spiritual guide and counsellor, dialogued with me over the years, concurring with *Second Innocence* and reading the manuscript. He affirmed it deeply and wrote the foreword.

John McRae, founder of the Global Beacon Community of Prayer, read the manuscript and underlined the significance of friendship and universality.

In loving memory of my parents, the late Mary Burke McKillop and Tommy McKillop.

Fr. Tom McKillop, March 2008

Contents

Foreword by Benedict Vanier 13

Preface by Bill Wittman 15

Introduction by Fr. Tommy McKillop 25

1976 37

1977 77

1978 165

1979 197

1980 207

Funeral Mass of John Howard Griffin 215

Afterword 225

On the Trail of a Photograph 225

Recognition 227

Youth Corps 228

Foreword

This book is witness to a special friendship, warm and enduring. Back in the '70s, Fr. Tom would come here to the monastery with groups of Youth Corps and the two of us would go for long walks in the woods. Twice they came with John Howard Griffin. It was a marvel to see these two men together.

Tom, big, strong, sensitive and reflective, buoyant. John Howard in a wheelchair, shrivelled and crippled with pain and suffering. Present. Totally present.

Later I learned of those long, long, long-distance calls, Toronto to Texas. Tom was there, really there, quiet, nearly silent, present to John Howard. John Howard, paining and gasping in the suspense of the spasms, only half-there, for every breath.

What does that say? What does that mean? It means two men of heart and soul, deeply together in twin-suffering. Friendship.

We speak of the Foreword to a book – the word that "comes before."

Here I would like to speak of a "Forward." Reader, go forward. Go ahead, into "Friendship and Second Innocence."

Benedict Vanier
Cistercian Abbey
Oka, Quebec
November 2007

Preface
Through the Photographer's Lens

Image #1 – Tommy McKillop

I easily remember John Howard using the name "Tommy" when speaking with or of his friend Tom McKillop. Sometimes John referred to him with a smile as "Irish Tommy."

As far as I know, only John Howard called him "Tommy." Most of his other close friends and acquaintances called him Father Tom; Big Tom; Tom; Thomas; or Father McKillop. While all these names are laden with endearment, Tommy has surely become the preferred namesake. Perhaps it originated in his childhood, with his mother, Mary, and his father, Tommy. Perhaps John's personal use of "Tommy" in naming his dear friend began when he met and photographed Mary McKillop in the hospital shortly before she died.

John said Mary and he talked of her son and the deepening friendship between the two men. Perhaps at this sensitive time the intimacy of "Tommy" became a further sign

Fr. Tom's father, Tommy McKillop

Friendship and Second Innocence

of the depth of their fraternal bonding. I will choose this reason, although I'm probably still short of the full richness.

In June 2003, Pelletier Homes – a Toronto resource for young women who are re-establishing their lives – dedicated one of its residences to Tommy in recognition of his seminal efforts and support of his friend Gerry McGilly during the founding of these embracing abodes. The dedication plaque reads: Tommy McKillop Residence. The name is layered with precious meanings leading back to family.

Tommy's mother, Mary Burke McKillop. Credit: John Howard Griffin

The last time I spoke with John, who knew his health was profoundly failing, he told me to take care of Tommy. Over the years, my wife, Peggy, and I have tried to be responsive and friends to Tom, but never to the depth of John, his abiding friend ... of pure gold.

Image #2 – My First Meeting with John Howard Griffin

In early 1972, Father Tom gathered with Jean Vanier and others in Ottawa to discern better ways to reach youth with the Gospel message and inspire them to bring the Good News to the world. The following weekend, Tom met with Jesuit Father Bill Clarke, Sister Margaret Rose and about 30 others for further reflection.

Jean Vanier

Preface

The location was Regina Mundi Farm in Sharon, Ontario – a haven of solitude and residence for the Sisters of the Good Shepherd. The group met in the openness of the Sisters' chapel. During the sharing and discernment they centred on the family as the fundamental channel for transforming lives. Sister Marilyn Mangen suggested having family camping weekends at Regina Mundi Farm. The gatherings, to be called Christian Family Peace Weekends, would join families and strengthen them in the life and teachings of Jesus.

From this inspiration, the generosity of the Sisters and a sustaining core of volunteers, over a hundred Family Peace Weekends were held. As they evolved they included opportunities for fun and friendship; time for input and reflection on the Gospel message; and encouragement – a commission-

Fr. Tom McKillop celebrating Mass at Regina Mundi Farm in Sharon, Ontario. He is wearing the "People Chasuble," which is covered with faces.

ing to become families and people of action – to go forth into the world. During the 1970s and 1980s, thousands participated, coming as family units, or support groups, or individually. There was a great diversity of age, ethnic and cultural background, and physical and emotional abilities. All were welcomed and nourished. At a Christian Family Peace Weekend, you were sure to meet someone interesting. Many people became ignited with a passion for the Gospel during these weekends and to this day continue to spread the Good News. In 1977, Peggy and I met Father Tom through our involvement with COR weekend retreats* and our parish youth group. At that time Father Tom led Youth Corps – an archdiocesan team of young adults and others dedicated to building and inspiring faith and leadership in young people, with a focus on peace and justice. Tom was also deeply committed to the Christian Family Peace Weekends; he encouraged us to attend a weekend in June, adding that John Howard Griffin, the author of *Black Like Me*, would be present. Although I had not yet read Griffin's award-winning book, I knew that he had dyed his skin black and travelled the American South to experience the prejudice against persons who happened to be born black. The book's impact had been electrifying. I looked forward to being in the presence of this celebrity.

Photographer Bill Wittman with daughter Sarah.
Credit: John Howard Griffin

---

* The word COR (Latin for *heart*) stands for "Christ in Others Retreat." This movement began in Indiana and spread to Canada in the 1970s. COR weekends were designed to involve young people in a new, challenging approach to their faith and daily life as Christians.

After Peggy and I and our three girls – Judy, Nancy and infant Sarah (Rachel would be born five years later) pitched our tents, I set out to explore the farm grounds. On rounding a corner, about 25 feet away I saw a group of people clustered around a man in a wheelchair. Someone near me said, "That's John Howard Griffin." I was thrilled – there was the great man! I briefly wondered why he was in a wheelchair. I thought he might be recovering from a broken leg or some such inconvenience.

I determined to make a photographic record of my good fortune. I attached a telephoto lens to maintain a discreet distance, made a composition and pressed the shutter release once, and again, and again. Three times. Griffin must have heard the clicks, or perhaps his instincts alerted him to my presence. He looked up and motioned for me to come over. My heart froze – was he upset? Did he feel I had violated him by taking photos without permission? After all, he was an important person. Perhaps I had created an incident that would destroy the weekend!

I slowly walked over with feigned confidence. "Hello," I said. "How are you?"

"Fine," he replied. Then, "What film are you using?"

I wondered if he would ask me to give him the roll of film. I told him I used Kodak Tri-X, a professional black-and-white film. He indicated a preference for other Kodak films because they were less grainy. He then asked if I developed my own film. Yes. Do you have your own darkroom? Yes. What chemistries do you mix? In what quantities? My fear left me. We had a common interest. He knew and appreciated the alchemy of photography. Even better, John Howard wanted to share with me. I began asking about his own approaches to the craft. Soon we were exchanging fragments of information on chemicals and temperatures and secret techniques that promised to recover underexposed negatives or prints. We told stories of making favourite photographs. I soon realized that he was an accomplished photographer. In fact, he was a person of many accomplishments and abundant interests. I think the others who were there became bored with our inaccessible conversation and began to drift away.

We continued talking for a while. I was having the best time. I believe John was also enjoying the conversation. A moment leading to friendship. What a start to the weekend.

✸ ✸

Image #3 – My Favourite Photographs of John Howard

Bill Wittman at Regina Mundi Farm. Credit: Nancy Wittman

It was Fall 1977. Peggy and I were facilitating a Youth Corps leadership weekend at Sharon. John Howard was with us, actively engaged with the young people. During one of the skit presentations, something captured his attention. He raised his Leica camera to make a record. I was attracted to his movement – the expression of his creative energy. I quickly fo-

cused my camera on him. Four rapid images were made. I was satisfied – delighted! You can see the results above. I wonder if John's photo worked out as well for him.

Image #4 – The Tenderness of a Friend

In June 1978, we were back at Sharon at a Christian Family Peace Weekend. It was breakfast time, around 8:30 a.m. I was with Father Tom in the main place of gathering, Vanier Hall – a large room filled with tables and chairs, friendly, sometimes intimate chatter, and children running about. All central to the Sharon experience. Tom invited me to come with him as he went to help John Howard get up. John was staying in Good Shepherd Cottage, a small white wood house near the Sisters' residence. I recall a bright, uplifting morning. It was a short walk to the cottage. As we entered, almost silently, it was surprisingly dark inside. There was old, soft furniture in the living room. Pictures and mementos hung on the walls. In the shadows were interesting pieces of this and that – an organization of items common to the eclectic nature of rural cottages. Father Tom quietly knocked on a side room door, on the left. There was a barely audible response. Tom went into John's room while I remained in the living room looking at the various artifacts – some of which were historical.

I heard the two exchange a few words. After a short time I was invited to join them. The room was quite small – dark and sparse. John was still in bed. It was evident that he was uncomfortable. Tom began to gently – tenderly – massage John's heart. Then he moved to John's feet and calves to encourage circulation, which diabetes and heart disease were relentlessly attacking. After a while Tom's sensitive and caring efforts began to help John feel less discomfort. As John gathered his strength we all three spoke

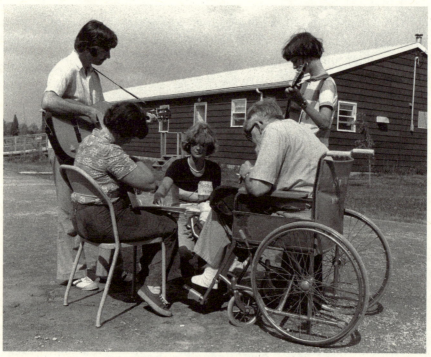

John Howard (foreground, at right) with a planning team at Sharon

of our weekend experiences, sharing personal and enriching anecdotes of our times with others. I recall John speaking of his conviction that the Sharon farm was a grace – an extraordinary place of hope where all were brothers and sisters.

What a privilege to be in this tiny room with these two – a gift!

Image #5 – The Last Meeting

It was early September 1978. Peggy and I were working with the Youth Corps team planning a series of leadership weekends for parish youth groups. To add a bit of fun to one of the planning sessions, Tom suggested a barbecue at our home. John Howard was in town and could join us. Peggy was excited at the prospect and wondered what John could eat, for he was on a restricted diet. Tom said yogurt would be perfect – preferably Astro yogurt, John's brand of choice. Peggy was able to purchase a container of it.

On the night of the meeting I left work and met Father Tom and John Howard at Bambi and John Rutledge's home in Toronto. Tom drove the three of us to Mississauga. We had a wonderful trip, enjoying small talk and sometimes memorable exchanges. We arrived at the same time as several members of the Youth Corps team and settled in with a light beverage.

Suddenly John Howard experienced chest pains. He took a nitroglycerine pill to ease the angina, to no effect. He took another. The pain worsened. Tom quickly took him outside and laid John on the patio table. Tom requested we not be present; he began pounding heavily on John's chest in an attempt to re-establish John's heart rhythm. Peggy and I were greatly afraid, as were the others. We called a doctor friend who recognized the complexity of John's multiple health challenges and told us to contact

John's doctor in Fort Worth. As we scrambled to discover where that phone number might be, Fr. Tom told us the crisis had passed. John Howard returned to the family room, quite weak from the ordeal. Tom asked Peggy to make some strong coffee cooled with ice and served without sugar or milk. After this was done it was decided to take John back to Bambi and John's, where he could rest. He flew back to Fort Worth two days later. The gathering was over. We had seen John for the last time.

Bill Wittman
Photographer
October 2007

Introduction

John Howard Griffin (1920–1980) is famous for being the man who chemically changed his skin colour from white to black in order to spend six weeks discovering firsthand how black people were treated in the southern United States in 1959. His bestselling book *Black Like Me* (1961) is a brilliant reflection on his experiences and on the attitudes and prejudices of that society. (Readers who are not familiar with this inspiring book are encouraged to read it. It is still in print and is available in over a dozen languages.)

Through that book, he shattered stereotypes and made countless people think twice about what it means to be human. And yet John Howard Griffin was so much more than the man we meet in *Black Like Me*.

John grew up in Texas. At the age of fifteen, he went to France to study French and literature,

This self-portrait shows John Howard Griffin at the time of *Black Like Me*.

then medicine. He was a gifted classical musician, studying under Nadia Boulanger and Robert Casedesus. His specialization was medieval music, especially Gregorian chant. Beginning when he was nineteen, he worked as a medic in the French Resistance army, evacuating Austrian Jews to safety from the Nazis; he then served in the US Army Air Corps in the South Seas for over three years during World War II. He was disabled in the fighting. After his release from the army, he studied philosophy and theology. Due to a shrapnel wound, he lost his eyesight in 1946. (He would regain it ten years later.) He converted to Catholicism in 1952 and became a close friend of philosopher Jacques Maritain, theologian and philosopher Father Gerald Vann, monk and educator Father Dominique Pire, and Thomas Merton. He took vows as a layman with the Carmelites.

John published four books while blind. His first one, a novel entitled *The Devil Rides Outside*, was a bestseller. In 1953, he married Elizabeth Ann Holland (he called her "Piedy"), who had been his piano student and was fifteen years his junior. They had four children: Susan, John, Gregory and Mandy. After his sight was restored, he became a professional photographer. He was also a gourmet cook.

For ten years, following the publication of *Black Like Me*, John travelled around North America and Europe, sharing with huge audiences the message of his insights on how the black man was being treated as an intrinsic "other" simply because of the colour of his skin. It was at one of these talks, to students at Michael Power High School in Toronto, that I first saw and heard John. He wore green-tinted glasses to protect his eyes and spoke with enormous magnetism. Every person there was riveted by the realness of his stories.

In 1964, he received the first annual Pacem in Terris Peace and Freedom Award, in commemoration of Pope John XXIII's 1963 encyclical, *Pacem in Terris* [Peace on earth]. The co-recipient that year was John F. Kennedy (awarded posthumously).

Introduction

A Youth Corps Leadership weekend at Sharon

I was a priest in the Archdiocese of Toronto by then; in 1966, I co-founded ("with Jesus") the Youth Corps, a church-based movement welcoming young people of all faiths. The goal of Youth Corps was to bring young people together to help the most vulnerable members of society and also to reflect on the world around them.

Dr. Wilson Head, a scholar from York University and a Quaker, played an important leadership role in Youth Corps.

Fr. Tom McKillop and Wilson Head

Friendship and Second Innocence

Robert Morgan, a performer who used theatre to work with people with disabilities, was also very involved.

As part of the program, young people attended lectures and presentations by leading Catholic thinkers and activists who were making a difference in the world: Jean Vanier; Dorothy Day; Cesar Chavez; Fr. Dan Egan, the Junkie Priest; Dom Helder Camara; Mother Teresa; and many others.

Robert Morgan performs at a Youth Corps event.

Cesar Chavez with John Howard Griffin.
Credit: Tom McKillop

Dom Helder Camara and Tom McKillop at a Youth Corps Event in 1985

Fr. Dan Egan, "The Junkie Priest," speaks to young people

Introduction

In 1968, I invited John Howard to come to Toronto and speak at Convocation Hall, University of Toronto. The impact of his words on the crowd was enormous. Inspired and moved by his message, I travelled to a number of cities and university campuses to hear him again and again. Often I would go up to him afterward and we would talk for a while.

In 1974, I invited John back to Toronto. He now sported a beard and used a wheelchair: his medical problems included diabetes, paralysis of the legs, a heart condition, cancer, and loss of one leg above the knee due to gangrene. After the presentations to the young and the old, we visited my mother, who was dying of cancer in Our Lady of Mercy Hospital. We then went to experience the Christian Family Peace Weekend, a family retreat experience in Sharon, Ontario. He told me he felt that he had discovered Eden.

John Howard Griffin at a 1968 Youth Corps event

Families shared conversation and meals at the farm in Sharon.

Friendship and Second Innocence

I received a letter from him a few days later.

June 11, 1974

Dear Tom,

In great haste to thank you and all of your colleagues for the overwhelming experience of being there with you and learning some of your activities, and the activities of others in that area. It was truly one of the most hopeful things I have seen in a long, long time ...

I will write you in more detail soon, but for now, I just want to say how happy and how moved I am by all of this, and quite especially by the book (I did not open the package until I got home) which all of us here will always treasure.

Your mother's beautiful face haunts me still. We are praying.

John Howard Griffin (third from left) and Tom McKillop (far right) in a group discussion at the farm in Sharon.

My wife and children were so excited about the things I told them, especially the experience at Sharon. We sat up and talked about it until almost 2 a.m.

Give all our friends there my warmest regards. I will get the photos to you as soon as I possibly can.

Yours ever in Christ,

John

Introduction

* *

Over the next year, the thought came to me time and again that I should make a retreat with John Howard at his home in Fort Worth, Texas. I had met someone I could tell everything to. Though at this time I did not know him well, I trusted him totally. Thoughts he had written in a letter to me early in the year stayed with me, nourishing that sense of connection:

January 3, 1975

Dear Tom,

Early morning – those hours before dawn that we did not get to spend together but in which I often think of you. I have received a most beautiful letter from Fr. Jim O'Donnell, telling me about your day together on December 26.

Fr. Jim O'Donnell

What a blessing you must be to one another. This kind of relationship becomes the more cherishable because of its extreme rarity in these days. I am going to send along the carbon I stuck in when I wrote him earlier this morning ...

It seems strange to be sitting here writing you when I feel your presence so much in these hours – as though I were writing to a friend who was seated right here in a chair beside me. I pray that you are well and happy and at peace. Our best love to you, to share with your colleagues there.

Yours in union with Christ,

John

✶ ✶

We decided I would spend a few days in Texas. I stayed with him and his family; he and I met whenever it was practical during the day. John didn't feel he was helping me, but I absorbed every insight and wrote each one down on the inside cover of my bible when I was alone. Sadly, I later misplaced that bible and never did find it again.

John Howard wrote me a letter expressing what he considered to be the meaning and grace of the visit.

October 16, 1975

Dear Tom,

You are on your way now, and I have just read the remarkable and beautiful dedication in the Quoist book you left with us. Thank you! I cannot imagine that anything in the book could be any better than your contribution.

Reflecting on your visit, I can only say that I have always cherished what you are, who you are and what you do. Now, because of the things we shared, that feeling is vastly deepened and I feel a great blessing came over our house and personally into my life, for which I feel nothing but gratitude. This has been something very special to me, far more than I could ever articulate. I know that the core of it will not be made known to others, for reasons that you fully understand. Most of it will never leave me at all. It will only strengthen my prayers for you as you pursue a life that I can now more fully share. I cannot for a moment doubt that you were sent here by God. Even a soul dedicated to solitude with God sometimes longs for this kind of companionship. With the deaths of all those close to me in this way: Tom Merton, Jacques Maritain, Gerald Vann, Robert Casadesus, I had perfectly accepted the fact that there in those places of the profoundest intimacy I would go on alone and without this kind of comradeship. So, although I am mute about such things, very quickly after your arrival I was aware that God was blessing me in a way that I had never anticipated and for which I would never think of asking. I trust that you detected all of that, though I could not say it.

I will not scruple about the fact that I felt you came here for something that I could not possibly provide and that I failed to provide. The consolation for my lacks in this direction is the certainty that dusts and muds of this poor soul were accepted by you as though they were of value, or at least they were accepted into your affection; and what a blessing for me this charity of yours that did not exhaust me by obliging me to try to be something I am not. My one regret is that we did not have those early morning hours together as you asked and as I wished. Too many other things intruded and made me fail you there but you will be with me in spirit as I begin – or resume – that practice tomorrow morning.

Great love to you from all of us here,

John

Our relationship grew over time; we became brothers to each other. This was a rare relationship – a spiritual friendship, the deepest and most intimate of my life.

Over the next five years, we wrote back and forth often, telephoned, visited, worked on common projects and sent audiotapes. John was increasingly ill. He was experiencing much pain and spiritual desolation. I responded to him in his vulnerability; he coached me in my spiritual journey.

A year before John died, we planned the homily for his funeral together. Two weeks before he died, I went down to the hospital in Fort Worth to live beside him for eight days. These were days of great pain and suffering for him. He died a week after I left.

Piedy asked me to celebrate the funeral Mass and deliver the homily. Paula Kriwoy and David Graham, two young friends of John Howard's, came from Toronto to sing at the Mass. Gerry McGilly, a great admirer of his, came to lend his prayerful and loving support to the family.

David Graham singing and playing at a Youth Corps gathering

This book is a collection of letters and fragments of letters from John Howard Griffin to me, and a few of his journal entries, along with my letters and reflections to him. (My letters to him were misplaced for a number of years. His wife, Piedy, found them and graciously returned them to me.) All were written between 1974 and John's death in 1980; most are dated 1976 to 1978, when our correspondence was at its peak and before John's health began seriously to decline.

I didn't intend to publish these pieces, but when I organized and reread them I felt that here was an experience of spiritual friendship based on "second innocence" that deserved a wider readership. As John put it, "Each of us begins as a child, innocent; each of us as an adult must come to a second innocence, where you know and experience evil and you choose to be childlike." He wrote near the end of his life that, for him, life was reduced to two words: love and innocence.

Introduction

After speaking about these rare letters to Bill Wittman, a friend and colleague who did the photographs for my earlier books – *What's Happening to Me? A Teenage Journey* and *What It's All About: Youth in Search of Meaning* – he encouraged me to share them. I promised I would; this book is this result.

The words found in this book are precious, delicate, intimate. I hope you will find them insightful and nourishing for your own life.

Fr. Tom McKillop
Toronto, Canada
June 2007

1976

Friendship and Second Innocence

January 3, 1976

Dear Jim,**

Your letter of December 30 is here before me, next to this typewriter. I have read it and reread it and prayed over it and for you in these early morning hours before dawn. I, too, share the feeling of closeness with you and with Tom that you mention – a sense of profound union of prayer and concern and affection that makes us closer than brothers even though God never grants us the joys of seeing and meeting one another. That there can be this kind of union of souls without impediment and with nothing that will be judged or needs to be hidden is, as you say, a great blessing from God. In our world today, even among men of the spirit, it is rare, though men long for it and speak much of it.

What you tell me touches me deeper than I can say. In a sense we move somewhat in similar directions. I can no longer be there physically among the poorest of the poor, though I spent many years learning the meaning of Bloy's contradistinction between poverty and misery: and I think that when you speak of the poorest of the poor, you are talking about human misery. For weeks now I have been writing in this area. God apparently wants this of me, since my situation has been so arranged that I am physically blocked from doing anything else. In a strange sense, at the human level, perhaps I am so moved by your letter and the apparent direction of your vocation because you seem to be moving toward doing what I can no longer do – and there is that vast need out there: not so much for "change," not so much for action that produces "measurable results" (you will hopefully never want to see any results), but simply for the balm of Christ's love and sharing in the lives of the miserable that so long for anything healing, sane, dignifying.

There is also a feeling of dread for you. I don't want to be a burden to you. At my levels of misery and humiliation, a man has got to be deeply wounded and

---

** This letter was sent to Fr. Jim O'Donnell – later the founder of the Little Brothers & Sisters of the Eucharist in Cleveland, Ohio.

stripped of all ambition before his presence is truly healing. The world is full of fruitless efforts to "help" the other without becoming the other. So in a sense I hate to see you as a friend go through this. One has to undo so much that has become natural in our lives – one has to realize that when there is nothing to draw on (financially), the purchase of that book, or that movie ticket, or that trinket can be deeply scandalizing (if it is bought for oneself).

But you know all of that, and you know that in these areas, no one wants to hear words about Christ, one wants to see Christ living in you; one wants to see the overflow of Christ living in your actions. Merton's very last words before he died were to this effect: we must be so permeated by Christ that what we do will give the message without our ever needing to speak about it.

Thomas Merton.
Credit: John Howard Griffin

I pray for these things for you, and I will pray for you constantly and with all my heart, and much of those prayers will be prayers of thanksgiving that you exist and live what is humanly unbearable without an abundance of God's grace. In the deepest sense, if your experience is anything like mine you will find that you went among the miserable to console and to heal, and the miserable ended up consoling and healing you. But that may never be obvious.

Please do keep me informed and write me when you are moved to do so.

In Christ's love,

John

P.S. Later: I cannot get this out of my mind. I am timid about speaking in this way. I am suspicious of institutional or organized efforts in the area of human desperation – because it seems to me that these inevitably tend toward mediocrity, though that is not at all necessary.

I see all of this from the viewpoint of the victims of humiliation and misery who have seen so many good people come and go, come and never become one of them, come with programs that give hope and then vanish or die without ever knowing really why. In this kind of vocation, one has to remain somewhat unstructured, open to the movements of the Holy Spirit. Almost anyone less than a saint going into the world of the miserable is going to be considered a pest, although often a helpful pest.

The important thing is to let God do with you what must be done and never to take over and do it yourself. Over the long haul, this involves the hard and cold total sacrifice of self which sounds all right but is immensely difficult, though if one can persevere it succeeds in burning out everything except an infinite capacity to love. It would be foolish to suggest that this can be anything but terrifying at times. The tone of your letter and the direction your vocation has taken make me think that you have gone a long way in this unfettering of your capacity to love.

January 16, 1976

Dear Tom,

Snowed under with work. Oh, I have a new disease, or complication rather, and this should edify you. The other morning I woke up with a black tongue. Strange. Piedy got worried for fear it was my old condition of blackness coming back on me – or else, bubonic plague. I called the doctor and he explained that it was the side-effect of the antibiotics I have to take to save this foot, which now appears in real danger of being lost. It turned out to be a fungus caused by the antibiotic and is called aspergillus niger. The 'niger' is clear. The aspergillosis springs from the fact the spores resemble "the brushes (aspergilla) used for sprinkling holy water." I thought this was enormously edifying and proved I was a good Catholic, and told the doctor so. "Thank God, I've finally got something that is both distinguished and Catholic," I said.

He told me that it was rare, but not distinguished, since it is exactly what dogs get when we speak of "black tongue." Well, shucks again!

February 10, 1976

Dear Tom,

It is early morning as I write this note. I am listening to the Handel Concerti Grossi – wonderful and jubilant and sane music: I let that do much of my praying for me. God is certainly in such inspiration, God in an aspect of felicity and love. There are times surely when God must hunger for offerings of pure joy and pure beauty that ask for nothing, but just give. In a world and a time where we are surrounded by such massive and frightful moral, spiritual, physical and intellectual suffering, surely it is good to take a few moments in the early morning just to share something pure and renewing before plunging back into all those problems. I listen – more than that, I give myself to music so sublime it brings tears to my eyes; and glancing down see the notes I wrote yesterday.

> For minority people, the bitter deficiencies of the earlier years may limit their life expectancy. With advancing age, the severity of poverty is intensified and so is the sense of helplessness to do anything about it. Poverty of old age is often preceded by deprivation of adequate food, shelter

and income from birth. Since they do not fit into categories that serve the majority, service to them is limited or non-existent.

Love from all of us,

John

✶ ✶

March 2, 1976

Dear Tom,

Writing that salutation, I had the sudden and startling reaction that I had begun a letter to Tom Merton. Another quick reaction telling me that "Tom" was no longer here. Then the realization that I wrote that salutation for you and not for him.

I suppose all of that subconscious activity came from the fact that I have been preparing a lot of slides from black-and-white photos of Tom for my Merton seminars this spring. He was much in my mind.

Just as you have been. Luiz de Moura-Castro and Bridget came down for a moment yesterday and as always asked about you.

We all hope and pray that the period of hard suffering is now past and that you are recovering comfortably.

Our time has been spent mostly with my dad, who has had another bad spell with his heart. My brother and his family arrived from Venezuela and that has been a great good for all of us.

I have heard twice from John Girard. I think they are still at Christ in the Desert. God bless that little group of saints for having the courage to carry through with an attempt at such a difficult vocation. I hope the terrifying realities will not damage them. It takes truly heroic love to confront the kind of poverty they are going to face and share. Over the long haul, it makes love difficult to sustain.

All for the moment. I hope you are better now. Thank you for all your prayers and for sharing your suffering with us. My dad seems to be improving again, though he requires the most constant watching.

Love to you from all of us here,

John

March 24, 1976

Dear Tom,

In great haste to tell you that Fr. Augustine Healy, O.C.D., an old friend, offered to pick you up at the airport and deliver you to Mt. Carmel Center in Dallas. So that is taken care of.

Fr. Gus is from Brooklyn originally – a great friend. You will enjoy meeting him. He is Gregory's godfather, by special permission.

Bless your heart. It will be great to have you with me at Mt. Carmel.

Love from all, to you and our friends there,

John

Friendship and Second Innocence

April 14, 1976

Dear Tom,

A quick note to tell you that my dad died early yesterday morning, the most merciful of deaths, in his sleep and without agony. He waited until my brother and sister arrived from Houston, recognized all of us and then went to sleep. A few hours later he simply expired.

The funeral is today at 2:00.

Our love to you and all of our friends there,

John

April 21, 1976

Dear Old Tom,

Thank you for your marvellously beautiful letter about my father. I know that we are close in our emotions – I felt the equivalent when your blessed mother died.

After that good close week in Dallas recently, I find myself missing you. I have no one who needs my graham-crackers-cream specialty! Don't apologize for anything in Dallas – the questionings, etc. It was an unalloyed blessing to share that week in that beautiful quiet house of prayer with you. I was also very moved that Father Gus and Father Philip came to my dad's funeral. You left too soon. I went into an insulin reaction Friday afternoon, completely knocked out and blacked out. Got through the evening session God only knows how. All of the people who assaulted God with prayers the night before looked mightily perturbed to see me so ill. Father Antony – who asked to see me after you left, and who wanted me to help him with his "character problem" – said he was too "dago" and had been turned off by the previous night's praying, etc., and could I help him straighten out his attitudes toward such things? He was consoled that you had found it a bit "pushy" and perhaps moreso to find that, as I said, "Before I could help you with your attitude, someone would have to help me correct mine." My "group" did not come forward the second night to "insist" that God do what they wanted rather than what God wanted.

Luiz came in last night. Rave reviews from Rome. They immediately engaged him for a second concert next month, something almost unheard of in a major city.

We celebrated Easter here at home, with Fr. George coming to say Mass for us and Bridget de Moura-Castro. I have had to stay off of my foot, which swelled and broke open at the hospital but is rapidly getting better.

Piedy was an unbelievable angel during all of this, feeding over 40 people each of two days. Limitlessly generous souls are always astonishing, aren't they? What a beautiful thing to be married to one, and after all of these years to find new reasons every day to be thankful for her.

All for the moment, old friend. Much love to you from all of your friends here, especially from

Your brother,

John

June 16, 1976

Dear Old Tom,

In terrible haste this morning of my 56th birthday to thank you for the phone call.

Father George comes at 2:00 today to say a birthday Mass for me here in my studio. We will pray especially for all of your team and intentions and for you.

Everyone here sends great love to you. Please remember me to all of my friends there.

Yours,

John

September 13, 1976

Dear John,

Paul Woodcroft (formerly Fr.) would love to have you speak in Oshawa to members of the association on the area of the handicapped and suffering. That's my own interpretation. The spiritual life committee of the Archdiocese (priests) decided not to have you for the priests. They feel that your image (social concern) would not appeal and attract on the spiritual life. They must have felt that Jacques Maritain, Gerald Vann and Thomas Merton were not heavy enough as part of your life. This shows where we're at, especially when it wouldn't cost them a dime for transportation or expenses. The fear of failure still plagues even the spiritual organizer. I felt badly but Paul Woodcroft and those working with him want you. Sound familiar?

Fr. Tom McKillop speaks at a Sharon Family Peace Weekend

Racism is coming out of the mouths of people, even priests – sometimes as concern, more as jokes. At the present time, 75 have applied for the Seminar, 50 for the entire Institute, 18 for different nights, 36 for Racism and 16 for the weekend. Catholic high school principals are enthusiastic over your talk to students at Massey Hall (possible 3,000). Have until October 13th to sell tickets – will be surprised personally if jammed – but the leadership is enthusiastic. Also, the Commission on Racism is ready for you.

Rushing to a team meeting.

Sincerely in Jesus,

Tom

September 20, 1976

Dear John,

I was glad to get through to you. It's great that we were able to pin down some points.

1. Sr. Marguerite Davies, Sr. Gwen Smith and myself are going to work together as a team.
2. The dates are as we had originally – Monday, Oct. 25th till Sunday, Nov. 7th.
3. The place is St. Joseph's College School, which has a ramp and an elevator – no steps. Here you could stay, have meals and the Mass. There would be a good chance for privacy. We could pray together.
4. You would be assured of $2,000 plus expenses. The larger events would help to take the burden of the Institute, and all the money

after local expenses would go to you for people on organizations of your own choice.

5. The cost for the Thomas Merton Institute for the ten evenings including the Musical Synthesis by Luiz would be $15. Individual nights will be $2 each. These prices are based on the principle of making it available to as many as possible.

6. It will be called the John Howard Griffin Seminar because it includes Racism and Intercultural Communication along with Thomas Merton.

7. Would you please send:
   a) Glossy photos of Thomas Merton, Luiz Mauro Castro, John Howard Griffin
   b) Short biographical summaries of all three.
   c) Listing of books you would recommend reading:
      – Thomas Merton
      – Racism
      – If any – for intercultural and multi-ethnic communication
   d) A general description of the eight evenings or nine evenings (if ninth evening is on controversies, if that seems right).
   There was a hope that you might list the titles as guidelines for the individual evenings. This may seem like binding you, but it is simply to give a sense for those who might not be able to make the nine evenings but who could be there for three or four individual evenings. Please feel free in this!

8. The key thrust at the moment seemed to be the relationship of the spirituality of a monk to lay spirituality – his personal struggle with contemplation and action, solitude and social justice.

A Portrait of Father Thomas Merton by John Howard Griffin

The audience, from guesswork, would include people from university, from parishes, religious houses, charismatics, Sharon people and social justice people and groups, as well as some young people, especially for the Merton Institute.

The day schedule tentatively would be:

Monday, Oct. 25th – Arrival from Windsor

Tuesday, Oct. 26th – Free

Wednesday, Oct. 27th – Morning meeting with special ecumenical committee on Racism in the city

Thursday, Oct. 28th – Day with priests at Sharon. Morning session probably with you – time for prayer and relaxation there

Friday, Oct. 29th – Free

Saturday, Oct. 30th – Youth Corps leadership day with youth and leaders

Sunday, Oct. 31st – Luiz Mauro Castro arrives for one presentation

Monday, Nov. 1st – Luncheon meetings with students at St. Joseph's College – spontaneous questions – sharing

Tuesday, Nov. 2nd – Catholic high schools

Wednesday, Nov. 3rd – Large presentation

Thursday, Nov. 4th – Intercultural & multi-ethnic communication

Sorry if this letter is so organizational – but it is great to feel that we are finally on the way. Will write you more humanly beginning of week.

Love,

Sincerely in Jesus,

Tom McKillop

P.S. We are praying for you – especially on this Pentecost Commitment weekend.

October 8, 1976

Dear John,

It was good to talk to you today even for a few minutes. I'm really looking forward to you coming. We'll have the wheelchair ready and all the comforts of life except one! Up to the present moment which is 3:02 p.m. Friday, October 8th, there have been 132 applications: 69 are for the entire series of Thomas Merton; 40 are coming for a few nights; 57 are for Racism; and 24 are for Intercultural weekend. The key priests on the cultural and ethnic groups have each received a personal letter to come up with 25 key people for the weekend – it'll be interesting to see who does. With two weeks to go, it should be a great time of response and readiness for what is to come. I prayed for you early this morning and we'll be praying while meeting at 4:00 p.m. this afternoon.

I have my new suit on, navy blue with the shoes repaired and a new blue shirt. Staff members have to wear shady glasses today – a little too radiant and spectacular. I'll try to cool it when I'm with you in case they start to follow me instead of SOMEONE ELSE.

My next personal move is to spend more time at night praying. I tend to dodge that period, which is really crucial for me.

We had a week-long pastoral seminar on Christian marriage in the diocese. It was for the priests, headed up by a key committee. It turned out well except underneath it was more safe, protected, controlled so as not to cause division. I criticized it as programming rather than probing.

There have been breakthroughs on the issue of transportation for the physically handicapped. As a demonstration project for two years, they will receive transportation at normal cost for those included in work, medical need and post-secondary education. We have 37 going to night school this year.

We have 16 university students ready to enter into the private and family current scene, which means developing small teams to begin a contact within the detention home and build up a network around different parts of the university. The priests in the area of youth seem more interested.

There are less than two weeks left and I sense that Jesus will touch deeply those who are meant to be there.

Love from all of us, especially Big Tom.

Sincerely in Christ,

Tom McKillop

Montreal   November 12, 1976

Dear Tom,

Cold and snowy this afternoon as dusk becomes night at 5:00 p.m. I sit here in this dim light, silent after the great blur of appearances one after the other this week. Everyone has been wonderful. It is always deeply moving to see the kindness of people struggling to solve problems in a search for their humanity. I am numb and stupefied now that most of it is over. Tomorrow I have free to fix the foot and fix the side and clean myself up. I was supposed to go see Lanza del Vasto this afternoon, but had an insulin reaction from neglecting to eat and had to call it off – mercifully for him, I think, since everyone wants to see him.

Albert and Karen have been to nearly everything. I have been able to receive communion each day and that is a blessing. The doctor sent a prescription for the eye and was reassuring.

In bad moments, I have remembered that extraordinary last Mass we had and your prayers and your friendship – all a great gift to me. I wish we could sit together and talk as we did most evenings there.

I hope you are happy and at peace.

Much love, to you and all our friends there,

John

Rochester, N.Y. November 17, 1976

Dear Big T.,

How good to hear your voice for a moment yesterday. Sorry we could not talk more. I had someone on the other line about my flight.

I wish you were here. Rochester is difficult ... I am in a tiny overheated room in the school infirmary section of a large dorm; noisy as hell. The nurse offered to help me take my bath. Students knock on the door. After the grand times in Toronto and Montreal, this is a mess. I offer it up – grouchily.

Talked to Piedy last night. She says two "pilgrims" have called, eager to see me, eager to stay with us. I told her to tell them I could not see anyone for at least a month. Somehow this flood has got to stop. I feel half dead. I feel the need to work quietly, to shut up and be still for a while. You are one of those blessed ones who do not seem to disturb the quiet. You belong in that quiet part of me.

Later: Tried to rest, but am constantly interrupted – the doctor, the nurses, the P.R. man – all very kind and nice. Am desperate for some quiet and some rest. Radio and TV people are coming in a half hour – one at 10:45, another at 11:15.

I have made arrangements to go home Saturday, arriving at 7:35 p.m. I am to see the doctors on Monday. I can't imagine they will be happy. My feet are almost double in size. My abdomen pulled open again from the exertion of wheeling myself through the long miles of Montreal's airport.

Father just came for a short visit. I got him to show me how to crack the window here, so life is now less sauna'd.

All for the moment. Best love to everyone there,

Your brother,

John

Rochester, N.Y.   November 20, 1976

Dear Big T.,

Things are finally finished. All the students have gone home for the Thanksgiving week. I sit here in the deep silence of this room, surrounded by the empty rooms. It is snowing. The wind blows at my windows. The silence takes me and begins its blessed healing.

Friendship and Second Innocence

I went yesterday to lecture at the Trappists – very beautiful. Lecture here at the college – and then they left me alone. I read and slept and listened to the silence. John Eudes, the Abbot, gave me Henri Nouwen's *The Genesee Diary*. These lines made me think of you and me:

> This morning John Eudes made a remark about solitude and intimacy that touched me deeply. He said, "Without solitude there can be no real people.... the measure of your solitude is the measure of your capacity for communion. The measure of your awareness of God's transcendent call to each person is the measure of your capacity for intimacy with others. If you do not realize that the persons to whom you are relating are each called to an eternal transcendent relationship... how can you relate intimately to another at his center from your center?"

Shadows and Light
by Fr. Tom McKillop

One thing
That I have
Become ever
More conscious of
Is the incessant
Presence of
A personal shadow.
It's never Far Away
And seems
To lurk nearby

Sometimes during
The sacred moments or
After an extraordinary
High experience or When
the body is Achingly
tired or Frustration
has
Reached the boiling point
And is ready To spill over
The shadow's Almost as
An entrancing person
Seems to come Through
the Particular moment
The opening My
vulnerability And
then
After being Accepted
somewhat Even in the
Smallest way It
begins to Speak
quietly And
persistently Over my
imagination And I
sense That the
conquerer Is once
again Ready for
victory And I seem
Lulled into defeat.

There is a sense
Of being
On the brink

Close to the
Sharp edge
Almost destined
To be devoured
And there is
Almost a Strange
desire Of
surrender. The
return Over and
Over again Of
the
Evil one.
Is it really
Someone else
Something else
Or is it
My unmasked self?
I pray
To Jesus Simply by
Whispering His name
Yet there are Long
periods Where He is
There in
The back Of
my mind
I am conscious
But I seem
To be drifting
Vague in my
Divine Consciousness.

These are the
Precious moments
Of reading Deep
truths Entering
into A meaning
For the life In
someone Else and
in Myself.
I work, respond,
Press forward,
Feel the never ceasing
Magnet of
Trying to do
Good with God.
But once The
work is Stopped
and Solitude
and Silence
begins The
shadow Of death
Of sins Raises
its Ugly head
And what Was
not
Conscious suddenly
Becomes visible And
enveloping. The
least stoppage
Seems to leave The
opening For a
Coming defeat!

If I am
To remain Or
regain The light
In my Own life.
There is an
Inner struggle
An entanglement
With inner And
outer evils I
get
Worn down
Feel weak
In prayer
In temptation
In strength
And I need To
turn
To someone else To
share what Feels so
delicate. So tender
And for it To be
received As
something Aching
and Paining.
So few
Perhaps only one
An intimate gift
Of a friend's heart
Receiving it Is
like pouring
Garbage into a
Spring and The

purification Has
again Taken place.

But sometimes
There is
No one
Of that quality
Nearby and I
turn to A
brother To not
only Receive the
Inner secret But
to
Speak to me
And to my heart The
words of Jesus "I
absolve you – I
forgive you I love
you" Joy fills My
soul
And I
Am lifted ?
Up made
Lighter conscious
Of being Free
again Though the
Shadow seems To
lay low And comes
again In the
future To tempt To
seduce To entice.
Yet the

Sacred moment
Happens and I
can speak
Jesus' name
Again not only
On my lips
But from the heart.
I am absolved I am
forgiven I am loved
I love you Jesus I
can
Love myself
Again more
Freely and
Love others
With even
More compassion And
understanding. I
believe but Do not
see
The darkened shadow
Feel the impending
Defeat bias At
times like This I
believe But do not
see But experience
The lightened
Realness of Jesus
The renewal Of
myself The healing
Of my heart.

✶ ✶

December 3, 1976

Blessed Tom,

I realize now what a great glory is this kind of union of hearts and minds. For many years I have lived in a great loneliness in my deepest self, satisfied for that to be an area inhabited only by Jesus. I would have accepted that forever and had accepted it. Now, in ways I do not even try to understand, you have come into these depths as a confidant and beloved companion. It is a gift beyond imagining for me, deeper and purer than any I have ever known. It allows us to be as free and unmasked with each other as we are with the Jesus within us, without any fear that our faults will make us less loved by one another, without any fear of offending one another in what we do or say. I feel immensely supported and strengthened in all of this and I pray that you do, too.

John

December 12, 1976

Dear John,

The tape you sent gave me some thoughts about the different kinds of relationship we have with each other – father, child, companionship, brother. It gave me some understanding of our approach of love to one another – maybe why I like "Tommy" or call you "Johnny" – how we flow in and out of roles – yet always towards personhood.

Friendship and Second Innocence

In the night
While eyes are closed A
voice whispers I love
you. A resonance comes
With bells and music
Interruptions and stops
Beginnings and again. At
first
I felt disappointed
With father and child
Child and father.
Then on listening more
Companionship and brotherhood
Came through in intimacy And
friendship. Your glorious news
Of freedom from Divine and
fantasy Reduced to physical.
I've felt myself The same
in sense Free to sleep
With movement almost free
Alive and yet Not trapped.
My difficulty earlier
Temptation to mirror
Short while Passed by
No sin.
Serious danger
Just floating Dangerous
in that way. Your voice
so rich On phone call
made Sounded ecstatic
Award caused joy A
little worry too.

1976

No need to be anxious
Money able to be given
To you without concern
Only care and love.
What is money But to bolster
A stallion who cannot race
Or do other things. Breathe easy, Pay the bills Get it together Space it out. Down the pills Climb the hill To sunlight
And health.
Your sense of self Sounds real and hopeful Your transparency A little worrisome
Unless you reduce the belly
Or stretch your clothes.
Glad to hear of Johnny's desire
To enter the real Touch the pain
Be present to you.
Heal, baby, heal
Father prays you well
Inside and outside.

Love,

Tom

✶ ✶

Friendship and Second Innocence

December 14, 1976

Dear John,

       I'm sitting in
       the poustinia
       for priests
       Called St. Eugene's.
       It's a square building
       made up of logs
       Cemented together.
       In front of me Are three
       things Hanging on the
       wall A rosary and Two
       Ikons, one of Mary and
       child And of Jesus
       teaching the inspired
       word. There's a scarlet
       Plastic glass with A
       bouquet of flowers Left
       by someone else. I have
       a small portion Of bread
       left An empty white cup
       A container of medicine
       And an oil lamp. My left
       arm is leaning On the
       first page of
       Ecclesiasticus And my cap
       The dark blue one Is
       sitting on the Sky
       blue linoleum Cover
       of the table. To my
       right

Is a bare red cross
And behind me To the
right A stove which
I won't be kindling
And then a small
Table and shelf With
necessities
For bathing, spraying
And a large jug Of
water.
I wrote a poem
On escapes,
Which I'll submit
In a shorter form
To *New Times*.

The bed has a
Board of wood as
A mattress. My
watch stopped mysteriously
At 2:40 p.m. This
afternoon.
This has never happened
So I am living in The
eternal now With the now
Growing darker with The
overhanging clouds. I've
been reading The Book of
Wisdom Which I really
hadn't Read in a long
time. I tried to relax
In the corpse position

For a long time To allow
the tension To go.
This afternoon
along with moments
Of prayer to Jesus
I fell asleep for a while,
Reading some of Catherine's
Poustinia. I have read it
before But it seemed As if
I hadn't Read anything. I
wrote her a Wee note
She is away with
Fr. Briere
Visiting some of
Her houses In the
States.
She is also speaking
To the Marianists In
Dakota. It started To
thunder A short while
ago and then stopped.
I talked for
A short while
To Mary Sallison. She's
at Madonna House For
the second time But
unsure what to do
Afterwards.
She's been living alone
Helping in the parish Getting
spiritual support From a
Benedictine. She speaks of

living in Colorado and going
wherever. She is a beautiful
person But needs a way And a
people
To integrate her life
Into the hustle and bustle
Of every day existence. It
is still dark But I'm up
Writing under oil light.
The bed was so hard I
hardly slept at all.

Love and Prayers,

Tommy

December 16, 1976

Dear John,

Day of recollection
Priests to come 22
Those who came 7
Later grew to 9
Reduced to 6 For
Eucharist.
Beautiful day
Evangelization in the morning
Hit on servanthood Direct
contact. Facts such
Sub-committee of Senate

Discovered of 40 parishes
Minimalism of visitation
Recommending all
Join your community of zero.
Social Planning I visited
Developed needs
No churches responded to survey
Showed resource booklet For
their own area Only 1 had it
By this time I was amazed!
Truth had struck For me
evidence beyond No
servanthood, no healing, no
contacts, no realness.
New Bishop ready with committee
Wanting Thomas for homilies
Ready again, Gestetner style To
be ministers of empty word.
Afternoon on inner prayer
Solitude, Reconciliation Film
Way Back Home. Excellent
Prodigal Son You could have
played All three parts – I'm
sorry Only two moving towards
The big Father – One ! Some
parishes still Socializing and
surviving Hanging on, covering
up Dying baby dying. All in all
Day was good A
privilege To
be there !

1976

Moving towards
A Gwen Smith insight
What we need
In challenge of life
Fill the vacuum Do it
on truth: Articles
focus Coming along
Margaret 'Communication' Gwen
'Awareness experience' Massey
Lombardi 'Interview person' Tom
'Poem on Forecast for Youth.'
Saturday ahead
Senator O'Connor teachers
Difference of Catholic System – Term
Spirit to influence – Mary Flynn
Connection with world – Gwen Smith.
Luiz and Claudette LeBlanc At
Maplehurst
Ave Maria, Mozart
Other heavier South
American Way. The
Lead spinning
Quickly today
Cresting in chaos
Of people, limited time.
Now spacing ready For
quiet Eucharist At
Dunsmere House Tonight
Am I happy
You ask?
Things, persons,
Going great. Prayer

continuing
Concentrated efforts
Thousand dollars Gift
for Trust Fund
Breakthroughs
Rather than breakdowns
The days ahead Filled
and packed Looking for
spare-time Week off
To breathe and relax.
A restless self
Calls to see
If parish life
Youth-wise
Goes on.
Will call more
Calling for life.
Jesus

Love,

Tom

* *

December 18, 1976

Dear John,

We prayed today
Eucharistically form
Thought of young deacon
Who died of epilepsy.

Priest with him
Feeling alone and overwhelmed
Three thousand families One
English-speaking priest Others
growing ill Hearts a-murmuring
Hidden ones a-fluttering
Weight growing heavy We prayed
for you Number 2
Only I knew your dilemma
Privates on the rocks Eskimo style.
What probably happens Is that while
others
Are speeding to the hot spots of the Caribbean
Your hot spot is being frozen. My only self is
trembling within The pace is slowly descending
The retreat House is soon I'm ready for quiet
and silence. Last commitments to Christmas Still
ahead to be done
Yet the strength will be given
I'm sure of that!
Thank you, Jesus, for life, love and friendship!

Merry Christmas.

Happy New Year.

Tom

December 27, 1976

Dear John,

I'm staying here at Combermere until January 2nd to rest, relax and pray for the new year. I'll probably climb some walls which I suppose you wish you had the opportunity to do.

Christmas was probably a precious time for you and the family – I hope it was.

My hope is that I may be more whole for the coming year – and I pray that you may be the same. Please give my love to Piedy, Luiz, Bridget and all the children including Admiral – I am so like him.

I wrote this letter about the Risen Jesus just because I felt moved to – hope it isn't out of place to share it with you.

Love,

Tom

Dear John,

I want to write to you personally – and intimately – about the Risen Jesus, who mysteriously dwells in us. There in the very centre of our being is the person of you, of me. At the root of your person and mine is the one whom you called Beloved, the Risen Jesus.

Rather than thinking of Him as statically sitting at the right hand of the Father, we should think of Him as not only present in the Father, but able to be present in each and every one of us. We believe that He can be in each particle of Bread and Wine through His consecration. So, too, He is within each of us sometimes consciously on our part and yet at most times unconsciously.

There in the depth of you and me Jesus re-invites you and me to come, to descend with our minds, imaginations, memories, with our hearts and our emotions down into the apparent darkness where the Light of Lights dwells. Flickering there by His Light is the tiny flame of you and me, sometimes glowing, at other times covered over to the point of almost going out. Yet He enlightens the darkness within and draws us within ourselves to the place where Jesus lives, loves, forgives, moves and breathes.

How frighteningly we stop from the busyness, the noise and fret of life to give the time, the concentration and the space to begin the descent. How easy it is to be caught by all that happens outside and inside ourselves as we are tantalized, seduced and attracted by what we see, hear, touch, remember and imagine. Everything seems to revolve around and on our head, or directed as our hands and feet are, by our needs and wants, our thoughts and desires. Only in silence and solitude with time and space pushed gently away can we slowly enter beneath to our heart, throbbing, murmuring, pounding, whatever yet slightly paining and through it towards that trembling nerve which vibrates with the emotions of unsureness, fear, fragility and weakness, tempting us to feel the hole of emptiness, the vacuum beneath. Yet down we must go, beneath the repressions and suppressions where tensions are taut, where breathing needs to be regained, where the person that is you and me begins to be more conscious again. How long is it that you and I have centred our minds, our hearts, our emotions, our Lord in our invisible yet tangible persons.

Through all the moments of life Jesus has been in us, knowing, experiencing, believing, trusting and loving each of us, and so often we have betrayed, denied, doubted, refused to accept the reality of realities. He loves you, He loves me.

Even when we float up and cover the Presence with our lesser desires, when we escape to the imagination, when we externalize the image and glory in the idol, there is a haunting sense of the Invisible One there down deep. No matter what expression or perversion we might turn to amidst the twisted moments of our passing fancy.

Immediately on sinning in our personal, not so unique ways, we are conscious of the emptiness, the escape from the real darkness where light has dwelt and draws us once again to descend within and to say, Jesus, Lord and Saviour, have mercy on me, a sinner. A period of gap is experienced; there is a sense of doubt. Does He love me still? Does He dwell within me even though? Has He forgiven me? Thank God for an external minister, a priest, to confirm His love, His indwelling, His forgiveness and to be the instrument of His healing power to you and me.

Risen Jesus, active within, whispering inaudibly by your Spirit. Jesus loves you and me. Jesus, you name me and flood me with your sense of peace. I am loved, yes, I am loved, yes, I am loved. How easy now comes Your Name rising to my lips from your person and mine, from your emotions and mine, through your pained heart and mine, with the whole of your heart and faculties and senses.

Finally, you and I express in an inaudible whisper the name of names – Jesus, sometimes Abba. There in the depth of you and me there is the growing conscious realization of the mysterious relationships with your Father and mine. Your brother and intimate friend and mine, your indwelling beloved Spirit who is your Lover and mine.

There is the internal presence of Love, which mysteriously still finds our extremities cold to His and then touches. It the source of creation, rebirth, reconciliation, creativity and friendship there in the centre of the depth of depths in you and me. But more than us, each and every one who is meant to be in our hearts – Pharisees, Sadducees, bigots, high priests, criminals, children, old forgotten ones, passing ones, bastards in our eyes, enemies at least in appearance.

There in the core of us is meant to be the mystical Body of Jesus in miniature, depending on the openness of our ears, our minds, our hearts, our emotions, our persons. Believable beyond belief is the Risen Jesus in you and me, but He is hidden within the other who is to be loved by you and me, as Jesus would love him or her. How far and yet how close we are to the growing conscious realization that the Risen Jesus is all in all beneath the distressing disguise of the other.

Remove the mask, go beneath the appearances, look beyond the cover, sink underneath the coldness, risk the touching of another and we find another fragile, weak, trembling person. There within the midst of the darkness of the garbage is the flickering flame of a sacred person, irreplaceable and unique, and in the core of that same person is the Light of Lights, the Risen Jesus, the Brother and intimate of you, me, him and her.

Love,

Tom

December 30, 1976

Dear John,

I went to see my family doctor just before coming here. Told him of the trembling body and the popping over one forehead. He checked the heart, looked at my chart and said that everything was beating well. All I needed was some tranquilizers for the tension. It has been a torrential wind of work and responses and I suppose that has something to do with my usual escapes now. I feel rather relaxed at the moment! The year 1977 is going to be a big one. I jokingly but seriously chided my Jewish doctor about all the Jewish people including himself who thought that I was trying to convert them when I invited them to hear Dr. Viktor Frankl a few years ago. I mentioned that he might be coming June 9th to Massey Hall. The chances are slim. He said no over the phone but said to write anyway. He said that he was 72 and felt that he could not inspire. I told him just to be there and he would inspire. (He is an immense perfectionist with an incredible ego but able to be melted.) If you haven't, you should read a few of his books – *Man's Search for Meaning*, *Logotherapy*, *Will to Meaning* and *The Unconscious God*. He is one of the commissioners for the Vatican. He has taught at the International U, in San Diego and at Duquesne in Pittsburgh.

Please pray for Old Tom.

Love,

Tom

1977

Friendship and Second Innocence

January 10, 1977

Dear Johnny Little John,

    Coughing air
While feeling the blues Ear
blocking the Bach You're
identifying too much With old
Beethoven. Hanky in drawer On
top drawer At least to have
The appearance of Following
your master's Direction in
this area.
The voice sometimes caravan-like
But your whispers always Asking
questions Searching and affirming,
Yet ever caring. Sorry for
misdirection On the Little Flower
Little Jesus praying for you
Probably roses will surround you
While the odour of sanctity grows.
In the days ahead When one becomes
more Wholly horizontal Peace flows
in a river Of suffering and
destination. Those who love you
Carry you and yet Challenge you to
get off Your Bell Telephone bottom
And move towards
The nearest one
The light The
Eucharist.

    Ahead is the Don Jail
The film with Bonnie

A fantastic lady with no arms
Yet spectacular in movement.
Tomorrow at Maplehurst
Tolstoy's "Martin the Cobbler" A
man who by his eyes And
expression reminds me
Completely of you. I only wish
that you Could see it
Where love is,
God is
A beautifully
Humorous
And touching
Discovery by the cobbler
Whatever you did to one
Of these, the least of my brothers
You did to me.

Keep breathing, Baby,
The Spirit breathes in you

Love,

Tommy

January 15, 1977

Dear John,

Silvano Salvaterra said that he wanted to move from convenience to commitment. The passage that really touches him is "Go sell what you have, take up your cross and follow me!" He wants to live a more intense Christian life – feels called to be a priest or religious – searching beautifully. A rare and beautiful gift! This year it's all going to happen (so says the prophet!).

Big Team reflection coming up Jan. 17th–19th – important time. Interview with Luiz Mauro Castro went sensational – it will be in *New Times* January 28th.

They chose my poem on youth over David Graham's because of the theme – Dave and I laughed a lot about it! He and Gerry are sending you a tape of their love!

Sincerely in Jesus,

Tom

January 18, 1977

Dear John,

It's around 10:30 on Tuesday evening and I've just finished a shower and I'm leaning back in the bed writing. The other members of the team are downstairs sitting by the fireplace. We've just completed two days of reflection and have scads of newsprint hung up on the wall with ideas printed with magic markers. We'll arise early tomorrow and try to pull most of it together by 11:00 a.m. We'll say Mass, have lunch and return home. Paula has kept the secret of her fiancé, John Girard, returning home. She didn't want to disturb the reflection and keep her mind on him. He's staying at my house. I left him a tape to welcome him home and expressed spontaneously a few thoughts on which to reflect. He'll probably have a difficult time for a while. Originally, he was going to stay with the team but suddenly he decided to come home. Part of it was the challenge of Paula who had given him up for a year. Part of him is probably back with the team in Cape Cod – it will be great to talk to him. That's probably the last thing he'll want to do especially if this means a series of talks with many people.

We used the Second Letter to the People of God from Taizé as a guide for us in our continuing growth in direction. I'll bring a copy for you when I come. I'll also bring *New Times*. It's quite good. Luiz Moura Castro should be in the next issue. I had an excellent interview with him. Dave Graham is having one of his poems printed for next time.

I'll give you some of the conclusions we came to when I arrive. I'll try not to burden you with such things – only if you feel relaxed – otherwise we'll simply share. We prayed for you tonight again. I'm really looking forward to going to you and the family. It's going to be an important gifted time – I'm certain !

The team is in excellent spirit. A young Italian, Silvano Salvaterra. His last name means saviour of the world – he is dynamite – a heart-afire free 22-year-old with tremendous presence and an extraordinary prayer life to accompany it. He is working with the physically handicapped children involved in what is called COR – Christ and Others on Retreat – and the Charismatics as well as the local Youth Corps group.

You sounded great on the phone. Time to sign off – the eyes are closing.

Love,

Tom

✶ ✶

John Howard Griffin
Diagnosed heart enlargement
Questions stir Heart murmur
or fluttering? Heart murmur
gives Thoughts of exhaustion
Overtiredness, tension Heart
crying for rest. Heart
fluttering means
St. Jerome's dancing maidens
Charley's angels Hidden
labyrinth, Hoping operation
horizontal
Doesn't always rise to the occasion
Otherwise heart fluttering Will cause
heart murmurs.
Physician speaks of preventative remedy
Sexual fasting and Jesus prayer Not much
of a choice For a spiritual person Like
our diocesan brother wanted. I guess it
just shows How social action
Always leads to Non-
spiritual sexist action. The
omission of they To let the
priest alone Certainly was a
Social sin of incredible insensitivity.
I had a Mass
Last night with young nurses
We prayed for you
Talked of presence and love. Heavy!
Bambi responded,
"We should phone René Levesque!"
My thought was to

Call Dairy Queen as a diversionary healing tactic.
Dixie Lee, walnuts and chocolate
A complete alternative to
Nightmare amours
We'll see how we can arrange it?
Last night, almost fell asleep In
front of a Sister talking Returned
home
Preparing for a recollection day with priests.

Tomorrow is the moment
Hope to remain inside –
Probably stutter on the big words
Evangelization, prayer and repentance,
New Times – find out Same name as
Communist International New Times – also
a name For a slick new magazine for *Time*
Begins Thursday.
Fans have already been turned on
To receive the barrage – at least a whimper
Copies will be sent to you. We tried to clean
up all the photos To keep you from riveting
Eyes and deepest self Towards the image.
St. Bernard – pure, murmur
But don't flutter – it doesn't flatter you at all!

Love,

Tom

February 20, 1977

Dear Tom,

I feel secure in the deep friendship that binds our hearts together and that above all is healing me. I don't think you'll ever know what a difference that can make in a heart victim.

John

February 20, 1977 (second letter)

Dear Tom,

Saturday night, I lay here unsleeping, exhausted but relatively happy and at peace. I was in that daze at the edge of sleep. A buzzard circled down from the sky and landed on my shoulder. It was the evil one. I looked into eyes bloody and devoid of any mercy. He terrorized me, telling me that he had me now; that Jesus had left my heart and that you had, too – gone on somewhere else, abandoned me. It seemed to last forever. I was paralyzed, unable to resist his words as he told me how worthless I have been, how foolish to hope for love – and that from now on it was between him and me.

I called several times during the afternoon and let the phone ring in your empty house, hoping the reserved Sacrament would hear the ringing from your little chapel. I let it ring and begged the Jesus in that tabernacle not to abandon me, to help me drive the evil one away. I did not expect to get you, to find you. I was surprised when you answered. In my mind I had been begging you to drive the evil one away, because I could not, I had no more strength. When you answered, I hardly knew what to say. You understood and prayed there on the phone and gradually warmth returned to this frozen soul. I knew only then that he was lying, that you have fled my heart in disgust, that Jesus had left me in disgust. Almost immediately afterwards, Father George brought me Communion. I could not talk yet. He sat there a moment and then left after giving me Communion. What was it? Twelve hours of the deepest agony and demoralization I have ever experienced. The shaking and the after-effects lasted until bedtime, but I controlled myself and my mother and Piedy thought only that I was very sick.

John

✹ ✹

March 3, 1977

Dear Tom,

This morning I was with you at 11:00 (your time) for that beautiful sharing of the Mass and a big kiss of peace, with all of the intentions from here going to you and your happiness and well-being, despite the discouragements.

John

✹ ✹

March 4, 1977

Dear Tom,

So sorry about John Girard's infirmity. Tell him I hope it is not too painful. The only time I ever tried that Yoga headstand, I overdid it (one night in Wichita, Kansas, when I was very exhausted and had to give an important lecture). I thought it might stimulate my mind! It so displaced my insides that I had to go to the hospital before midnight. I didn't tell them what I had done. They supposed it was an accident – a fall or something. This is what happens when a Good Christian fiddles around with exotic techniques.

John

March 6, 1977

Dear Tom,

Last night I recalled that one visit I made for the weekend in Sharon – how touched I was, how much I enjoyed peeling potatoes in the kitchen of that house with the ladies that night, how much I enjoyed that little room you gave me (at the end, off the dormitory).

Anyway, on this beautiful morning everything is pregnant (Bridget the goldfish) or getting pregnant (Serena the cat). It makes me feel horribly left out.

John

March 9, 1977

Dear Tom,

These pains and dizziness are bad signs, signs that something needs to be done – too much stress of some kind. For God's sake do not try to suffer them along. If it gets worse, then get on a plane and come here and rest and enjoy yourself for a time in an atmosphere where you are unreservedly loved, appreciated, honoured and cherished.

A love that can end was never really love in the first place, says St. Jerome. If it is great enough and authentic enough, then all actions, right or wrong, are taken up and dissolved in it.

John

March 10, 1977

Dear Tom,

Am still basking in that beautiful tape you sent and in the phone conversation last night. It seems to me that our relationship is now so solid, so safe and secure and so deep and so transparent that it is a bulwark for both of us against all the world's bullshit. It is truly a fabric sewn with the threads of freedom (to use a phrase I just invented), a protective mantle thrown over us by the love of God. Out of the quagmire of sickness and weakness comes a great deal of sunlight now. May it feed your heart with the same kind of healing happiness that I feel in my heart.

John

March 16, 1997

Dear Tom,

The psalms from today's Mass seem incredibly fitting. "Lord, pity me; I have no strength left; Lord, heal me. My limbs tremble, my spirits are altogether broken."

John

Friendship and Second Innocence

✶ ✶

March 17, 1977

Dear John,

I'm sitting in the Oyster Bar on Yorkville Street. It's a basement bar and I'm sitting alone at a table having a crème caramel and a glass of milk. Two characters are sitting ahead of me discussing marriage:

"Who wants to bring children into the world to simply fill it with WASPs?"

"You want children, she wants children. She wants to marry you – you aren't sure whether you want to be married."

"Right! I don't want to marry because I have a passionate hatred of women's lib – she doesn't really want children."

In the background, the music is flowing through, two young girls are finishing their dinner, the two guys are still rattling on while drinking beer. At the end of the room is a bar. I'm waiting for a quiet young friend, Frank Lynch, who plays the piano here and sings. He trained at St. Michael's Choir School since Grade 4, lived alone in the school, became involved in Youth Corps, wrote a series of brilliant folk and message songs, and played the guitar – but his great gift is the piano. I'm here tonight simply to support him. The conversation at the next table is rattling on.

"I tried to make her conform herself to my designs and will. She cried out for her own will."

It sounds so melodramatic as one is trying to advise the other with conviction. The atmosphere is dimly lit – a big Italian type is at the bar. Frank hasn't come in yet.

I just came from Emmaus House with Sr. Judy and the Sisters. We had a beautiful Eucharist - remembered you - feast of St. Joseph celebrated though it is St. Patrick's Day. It seems funny to be sitting here tonight. I read three of your letters which were in my inside pocket - I only had this piece of paper and decided to share these few moments with you.

It's after 9:00. Frank just came in. The crowd is older - there's a few Irish hats around. Frank is dreading playing a whole bag of Irish numbers. He's just sitting down and playing - a great gift. He's singing "Send in the Clowns." The girls are rapt listening - the crowd is rapping at the bar. Our friends next to me are still on the marriage bit. Frank is singing what they're wrestling or rapping about. It's a relaxing night.

I talked to Jim Corrigal, the pro football player who teaches at the Choir School. I've been meaning to speak to him about getting in better physical shape. He's drawing up a simple way of getting in shape. I started today by walking up to Ryerson College and around the square first. John Girard went walking with me. He advised me to go over to Eaton's and begin slowly after buying the toys.

Next to me - a single monologue of advice is still happening. "Things are different in marriage. It all comes out in the wash!"

Frank is moving into "Our Love Is Here to Stay." It's beautiful playing and singing. The girls have gone to the ladies' room. The marriage counsellor goes on: "Nothing is here to stay!" Waiters move around to pick up the dishes. "I had all the same worries as you have now!" The other smokes his pipe, listening to the avalanche of personal wisdom.

Gerry McGilly

We picked up 150 mattresses today: 50 for Sharon, 15 for Gerry McGilly's Jericho House, Assisi.

"Do you love her? Do you want to get married?"

John's cast is off now. He is starting a small business to be a helper! Music plays.

"Do you or don't you?" echoes next – while a couple are into an intimate embrace next to me on the left. They are holding each other while my milk is reducing in size in the glass. She giggles – he whispers – the noise surrounds the music. It's a job – long term – beautiful singing yet next to no one listens.

The girls return and walk out – say goodbye to Frank. He sings and plays "I Love You" while the cash register rings up. A waitress writes up a bill. The bartender in his leprechaun hat takes a swig. Frank sings, "I love you more!" The waiter walks down for more business – walks back.

The convention rolls on. "Nothing is black and white."

"To get the most out of the system you compromise; it's never what you really want!"

It's good to stop tonight.

"The point is – are you willing to compromise?" (another heavy question next to me).

"That's the way it works out! – that's what I'm trying to tell you!"

This all seems like nonsense – just a flowing of consciousness of an unreal scene. Frank just came over. Lovers now heavily loving.

Love,

Tom

★ ★

John:

> Mission of commitment
> Journey of direction What God
> wants and does Zig-zags and
> arrows, Black girl wounded
> Feeling isolation But
> heartening support And
> expression of love. Jim, once
> controlled Now vulnerable In
> the wiles of love And the
> jealousy of two. Pierced in
> charity With convincing words
> Deepened by experience Filled
> with powerful mystery. Eleven
> days of Holiness, nakedness
> Modesty, care
> And compassion.
> We part in flesh
> Yet live in
> Each others heart
> Of human flesh.
> A prayerful moment
> We live today
> Tomorrow to be taken care of
> We are one become One.

Love,

Tommy

✷ ✷

March 19, 1977 – Feast of St. Joseph

Dear Tom,

Listening to Bach this morning, trying to get some life into these veins and arteries; nothing comes. Even the great Passacaglia and Fugue produce no vivid stimulation. Nothing. I never prayed to be dead, Tommy, only to find the strength to resist temptation. Pray that some life returns to these bones. I don't mind being an ass, but I have strenuous objections to being a mule.

John

March 21, 1977

Confidential

    Mr. John Howard Griffin
    You have just been awarded
    This draft of $1,000
    For your extreme heroism
    And raw courage
    In the field of mass communications.
    Neither Evel Knievel Flying over
    sharks Or the beautiful girl In the
    plastic palm of King Kong Jack Ruby in
    dramatically Shooting Oswald in the
    jail Or Sirhan Sirhan
    With Bobby Kennedy
    Could outdo
    The fantastic, unbelievable
    Satyriasis of Satyriasisi.

> To allow yourself In your
> human condition
> To face Salome in her wiggling tube And
> with only the help of one person To
> undergo the movement of movements.
> Baptist lost his head de Foucauld died
> in the desert Andrew went out upside
> down But Griffin withstood
> Dramatically, humbly, Simply,
> metaphysically And came out of it
> Hopeful, peaceful
> Beyond the beyond.

The draft is real! So cash it and don't throw it away.

Sincerely in Jesus,

Tom

March 26, 1977

Dear John,

> Glad you received your award
> Otherwise you may have been bored
> With empty pockets and bailiff nearby
> The old dribbles would have been your last cry. The
> bed is filled with saintly St. Bernard Needing the
> spiritual direction of Admiral Cunard
> The shuffling shucks and grunting Oh's
> Leading you to releasing and expressing your Ah's. The

typewriter ribbon cut to shreds
Pounded by fingers, moved by thoughts, away from the dregs.
The heart flipping, turning to space and silence Needs a
celebrating host spirited to stillness Of
steadiness, balance, harmony and peace.

Love,

Tom

✷ ✷

Escapes
by Father Tom McKillop

Once there was
a statue of
an Israelite soldier,
looking towards the
Sinai Desert. Beneath
the statue
Were the significant words
"We looked at Death In the
face and Death lowered his
eyes." We feel awkward In
impersonal crowds, Or when
in solitary, not our
choice, At an airport,
International by name, I
arrived early to meet An
acquaintance by plane. I
did not know him well, But I

was asked to Pick him up.
His plane reported late
On the Arrival screen And
I began my movement In
midst of crowds Most of
who seemed
to have some connection
With sorrows.

I walked the length
Of the floor over
a score of times.
I stopped to buy
A large orange drink And
found it Nourishing, but
Lasting less than Half
the walk of The floor. I
noticed the face Of a man
midway Calmly watching.
An Italian family
Welcomed an older member
A little embarrassingly On
both cheeks One by one.

I noticed the California
Surf Team of Attractive
young men Wondering who they
were and where they were
going. I bought a newspaper
Just to fill up the time The
plane was delayed again And
sat wondering Through it.
I walked the length

of the floor And
bought an Ice cream
cone Patiently
waiting What else
was there To do?
I relished it
Though overpriced
At seventy-five cents
and carried on my Peripatetic
movement Consciously
restless. Finally the
plane Arrived and was
Noted on the screen Yet
the gap of time Seemed
interminable, For him to
appear. How difficult it
was To have the space And
time alone With myself.
How little I turned To
the Beloved within Or to
any one else In my heart.
I simply experienced The
ache of emptiness. Can I
live without Stimulus and
action? Can I be alone
Reflective, even lonely?
Can I be in solitude
Or must the self
Be surrounded by
Incessant music, noise,
Bustling, close friends?

Do I have to do
Something? – Telephone,
Drive, drop in Watch TV
Stand at a bar
Wager a bet.
Or is the moment Of
quiet, silence Solitude
too much With being too
little?
Do I sense semi-consciously
That death is nearby, In the
silence inside And I run,
run, run. Do I believe and
live Deep enough in Jesus To
stop, look at death And feel
that death lowers his eyes
for He has been conquered?
Often not!

March 28, 1977

Dear Tom,

Keep blessing me, old friend; keep me indwelling in your good strong heart – that is a home I love.

John

Friendship and Second Innocence

April 14, 1977

I read again and again the lines you scribbled at the airport especially: "Eleven days of // Holiness, nakedness/modesty, love/and compassion / we part in flesh / yet live in each other's heart / of human flesh, / a prayerful moment / we live today / tomorrow to be taken care of / we are one becoming One. //

John

✶ ✶

April 15, 1977

Dear Tom,

The news announced a British survey of women: the majority said that the naturally chubby men with thinning hair were their choice as the "best lovers." See, I told you. You'd better jog like hell, buddy and start using hair-restorer tonic – or you will be surrounded and overwhelmed by panting women!

John

✶ ✶

April 16, 1977

I think of you doing things, busy, healthy, in the presence of others, and sometimes wonder if they have any real ideas of who you are, what you really are. Certainly a few do. The ones who do are blessed.

John

✶ ✶

April 17, 1977

But my great hope is that if I die, I have time to call you and you would have time to be here to hold me when I leave this life. I have already accepted the sacrifice of that, because the chances are very small that you would be informed in time to come or even that you could come if informed. But the thought of that would make all the difference; it would soften the passing immeasurably for me. I really hope I can live, I keep hoping that, but until I have everything settled in my heart about the other, that remains the reality.

John

April 17, 1977 (second letter)

I still feel like a drowning man who grabbed at a life raft and somehow did it wrong.

John

April 18, 1977

We need to have Christ in the flesh, to touch, to tell everything to, to get it all straight and clear because we cannot do that entirely on our own. We need the Christ-brother, the Christ-twin, to keep us alive to the Jesus within who sometimes gets lost in all this anguished obscurity and confusion. You come to know that you can, if you ever get it all straight, that you can trust in love whereas you can never really trust in anything else.

John

Friendship and Second Innocence

April 21, 1977

How seldom in a human life can that total be shaved and embraced and made clean, without my role-playing (which is essentially lying), without any desire or need to manipulate opinion.

I cannot act what I am not (act brave, courageous, when I am being shredded), nor can I hide very well what I am. Only with you was I free to turn loose and be truthful and let you carry me and let you see my anguish and my tears – an incredibly blessed relief.

I was rather short with Piedy about not getting me the bandages. Turns out she got them two weeks ago, so that raises my percentage of screw-ups to about 92 per cent.

John

April 24, 1977

I explained to you that I told the doctor I would like to be kept artificially alive, if that was possible, and I could retain some consciousness – enough to fulfill my religious obligations and no longer; which meant long enough for you to get here and help me out of this life.

Piedy now knows a great deal about the true nature of our love for one another – not only through this but through other things I have told her and also about how your tape, for example (the last one) had such a transforming effect on me when I was so sick. All of this moves her very deeply.

John

**

April 27, 1977

At Mass today, I prayed deeply for a very special intention. That when I die, I be granted the special privilege of watching over you, of living on in my prayers and intercessions for you: (quite especially) of being always there in your heart to turn to, to remember; of being able even to make you understand how deeply you are cherished, of being more permanently present, more united, more watchful and supportive even than in life. Let me in my death keep open those floodgates of Jesus' love in your heart, as you have opened them up wide in my recent life.

John

**

April 28, 1977

The difference between me and the Pelagians is that I do not deny the existence of original sin, or believe that man can even achieve virtue on his own. My life has been a demonstration of that to me. But I do believe that he can do everything and usually more to open himself to God's grace – that alone can do it. That is why I become more and more convinced that unless we spend time alone with God, listening to the movements of Jesus within us, all the good intentions and free will in the world are really for nothing. That is why I am in an agony to get back into a state of grace when I fall.

John

Sharon, Ontario   May 7, 1977 (John's journal)

Tom will come soon and help me take my bath. He is the only person in the world with whom I can be truthful, be honest. But who knows what pain that causes him? He belongs in life. He glows in the presence of those young people. It is the burden of my death on him that worries me now more than anything. He says he thinks God is preparing him for that. He is a priest, but that is never enough. He is a beloved friend. That is the thing that makes his priesthood complete in relation to my dying.

Strange – at the end you have no great thoughts, only feelings, yearnings. You want someone you love to hold you. You yearn to leave life not comfortably – the physical agonies are not of any importance anyhow – but happily, being held, being embraced, being kissed by someone whose heart is part of yours. It has to be someone who helps you go without making you feel guilty for the sorrow you are causing.

Sharon, Ontario   May 8, 1977 (John's journal)

It is only at the end of my life that I have broken out of that inner solitude into an authentic community of love.

I have loved universally in nearly all my adult life – though guarding the secret within me of one unbetrayable love, whom I still have difficulty naming, whom I call the Beloved. Why can I not pronounce his name? Perhaps because I have heard it crucified and mutilated on so many lips that pronounce it easily, so easily the way you would say Bayer's Aspirin or Sal Hepatica and about as much meaning.

Later:

Role-playing such a love is the great lie, the delusion – it masks a million treacheries. Rather keep to the secret and the solitude then commit the blasphemy. I have never seen it even approximated in what we generally term "communities." Especially I have never seen it even nearly approximated in religious communities. That is no scandal. I have known it, at least in some authenticity with individuals in friendships. I have, in the last year of my life, experienced it finally in its completeness, in its true freedom and latitude, in its holiness and humanness, and only then have I been able to whisper the word "Jesus." Only then have I been able to make my confessions without unspeakable agony.

"He who lives in me and I in Him, will bear much fruit."

In this love you do not have to play-act, you do not have to say the "right words," you can finally trust your heart. The friend is born – perhaps the fruit is too abundant too suddenly after a life of hungering for it. Perhaps its greatness bursts the heart as the fish broke Peter's nets. No matter. It burst with joy and fullness. It is of such fullness that it can never befoul the beloved. It cannot be impure. It allows us to remove those psychological chastity belts which never even make us pure, truly pure, authentically pure. It ends that final role-playing. Those who are pure in heart – made so only by the love that lives in each other as it lives in the love of which Jesus speaks – only those no longer have to worry about "acting" pure. They finally are. There are no more laws – they don't need laws any longer. The "Laws" are part of their love. And the Gospels and Psalms burn like new words. They call us to life even in our dying.

I remember one thing vividly. A very secret thing: I remember dying one night, sinking, sinking out of life, confused but at peace with the terminations of my earthly existence – making the surrender. And from all of that vast obscurity, I felt an embrace; I felt two kisses. I was sure they were the kisses of the beloved and Beloved. They called me back from the darkness of dying peace to the light of living peace. They called me back to life. They were the unspoken words of the Beloved, saying, "Not yet for a while." My time was not yet. Only those two kisses let me know that. They were the only language my heart could understand. I do not know to this day and do not need to know if that really happened or if I dreamed it. It was the Christ action. I felt it as such. I am deeply grateful it happened for two reasons: it confirmed in the very fibre of my being that humans can finally fulfill that commandment to "love one another as I have loved you," and it gave me a few more hours, days, weeks – who knows? – to continue in life loving in that way in life.

No one should ever trust words to speak of such a mystery. No one should ever write "recipes" for achieving the experience of such a mysterious reality. It cannot be achieved. You can only hunger and thirst after it. When it comes, if it ever comes, it comes because the heart has been emptied of all impediments to the reception of pure gift. My life, in all its bungling and failure and weakness and vulnerability, has known this secret. I never even dared ask for the gift in earthly life. It came as pure gift. It is the final liberation. No one can really "deserve" it. It is pure gift. What can the poor recipient do there in those secret places that are no longer secret except weep? I believe this must be what is known as the gift of tears.

John

May 10 (over Chicago – John's journal)

If I am too stark, blessed, forgive me. When you get so near your last days you want to say things plain and bare and full of love – without any ornamentation, without any euphemisms.

I am too near the end to ration out my love or to ration the expression of it.

John

✶ ✶

May 11, 1977

Dear Tom,

I remember especially that sign in the chapel at Sharon – "My love endures to the very end" – and your words: "I'm with you all the way."

Personally, though – as one of yours – I cannot help but wish you could treat yourself a little more kindly.

John

P.S. You are the only one with whom I can share simply everything, with nothing held back. Somehow, even knowing what it costs you in prayerful anxiety, I cannot bear to lie to you, even to lessen your burdens. I pray that you will never be able to bear lying to me, even to lessen my burdens.

If I am in heaven then, I will do my damnedest to see that another "me" is sent to take care of you. These things have to be done out of deep and loving union, not as a duty. When they are done that way, they are a mercy to both the doer and the recipient of the doing.

One of my great releases and the flowering of my love for Jesus came long ago, the day I first discovered that you don't have to hide anything from the indwelling presence. I always use that criteria in measuring my love for humans. You are the only one who really fits it in all its nuances, and it is precisely in your humanity that I know it is possible to love another with this very pure but all-encompassing love of Jesus. I suppose that love for Him was the first great discovering of my life. To be able to love and be loved by you in exactly the same way has been the second great discovery of my life, though I always knew it was possible for two humans to do this, to become truly one becoming one.

May 13, 1977

Dear Tom,

I feel it came alive tonight – a real sense of Christ's presence in me, as though He made Himself fully felt after seeming to be so distant and hidden for a while. I thought of your beautiful expression that "Love is sometimes waiting, waiting for the Beloved, for some word or sign from the Beloved."

John

P.S. Fr. Jim O'Donnell said a beautiful thing – "Isn't it a blessing to be loved simply in your totality, in all your fragilities and weaknesses as well as in your strengths, as you really are, and to know that you are loved rather than some image of yourself being loved?"

Give your reality. You have known all the aspirations and failures and fullnesses and despairs that are real to your priestly vocation.

Astonish them by refusing to say anything that is not in your heart. When dark comes and you feel lonely and disoriented, as all of us do at certain moments, remember that you are never really lonely. Remember that you are in the right way, and in the end everything is finally worth all the bad moments. Even though my life becomes unbearable, as it has a few times, if I can live through those moments, almost immediately I see the blessings that were hidden from me while going through them.

May 21, 1977

Dear Tom,

You once said that you and I must help one another to be saints. In spite of all our faults, we must never lose that holy obligation of friendship and love.

As one who has ended up too often falling through into the waters beneath and temporarily drowning, I have some knowledge about how the heart can delude itself.

John

May 24, 1977

Dear Tom,

These lines from your note are beautiful. "A few roving thoughts / Of care and love / Experiencing prognosis of near death / Dullness or blindness / Taken away as mysteriously as come. / I/ For myself / A vicarious experience of your dilemma ..."

Father George came at that moment and brought me Communion. I took it with all my heart, praying for the report today, praying, "If it be near death, let me be with him. If it be deafness, let me live to take care of him. If it be blindness, let me live long enough to teach him how to handle that."

I am writing, asking for the time when I can call you, to find out what the doctor says. A phone strike there is maddening at such a time. Again, I think of your phrase that part of loving is waiting to hear, waiting to know. So I offer the waiting and the frustration and the deep anxiety for you, begging that the news be good, if that is God's will.

Take care, blessed Tommy, and take care of yourself. Not to follow the doctor's regimen because another time things seem more urgent would be a costly mistake for you now – a real sin since it would involve a kind of self-mutilation. I know how difficult it is to take the time from the things you love and are driven to do and for which you feel so needed. I know that such advice is difficult to follow. I failed consistently to follow it until too late and now I am paying dearly for it. This also is real, Tommy. All these things will make you feel so much better and ultimately accomplish much more for a longer time.

Psychologically it is a difficult time. It even becomes a time for blind faith and fidelity sometimes to see you through the vast temptations against your faith, your vocation, your work, the future. It is sometimes a time of religious slump. You get tired of the attempts to remain close to God. Jesus sometimes seems cold and distant in us. The secret is to expect this and understand it and not get panicky that it has all been a mistake and then try to make up for it with a more "integrated" or "humane" life as such great numbers of religious and priests are doing.

John

May 25, 1977

Dear Tom,

Right now I am up against a blank wall; I don't see any way out. I blindly offer all of this up, hoping that I will find a way. I let the pains and the frustrations and the loneliness and the uncertainties do a lot of the praying for me, but I feel absolutely bereft without the Mass – that is why most often these days sharing that Mass with you is really the high point of my days. It would take so little to finish me off now. The Mass is so terribly important to me. To miss it would be the last straw. I have long understood the essence of the gospels, but I have never had them burn me as now, never felt them so transparent in their nuances, speaking directly to me; never have they meant so much to my heart.

It is not that I am reluctant to die. It is that my willingness, sometimes desire, for death right now constitutes a thorough cop-out! An escape from problems that seem insurmountable with this weakening flesh. I offer all of this.

John

P.S. What really breaks my heart is that I so wanted to be a source of joy and peace and security to you and I will go on being a burden when you cannot really bear any more burdens.

May 27, 1977

I imagine you sitting on the edge of my bed, praying, holding your hand over my heart, holding me. That keeps me from getting too nervous. How I wish my head were on your chest. At that time I feel safe that way. Well, I'll get to bed and hope for the best.

John

May 31, 1977

I have always, since my early life, been obsessed with the need never to hurt anyone, especially those I love.

John

Excerpt from *The B.C. Catholic**

May 22, 1977, p. 2

Festival of Life
by Thurston Smith

The most eloquent personal testimony of the Festival was given on the opening night by *Black Like Me* author John Howard Griffin. Suffering from a severe heart condition and related disorders, he had come from his home in Texas "because what you are doing here is the one thing I would get up and come to. When I asked my doctor's permission to come he was rather amused that I was coming to a festival for life, for I would be the first to be put away by a committee for involuntary euthanasia," Griffin joked. He was going to talk in a way he had never talked before, he said.

"Since 19 years of age I have been tremendously preoccupied with those forces that dehumanize. And again and again I have seen the pattern repeat itself, with people who have not become sufficiently aware or informed in time. I have always been struck by Edmund Burke's saying that all that is required for evil to triumph is for good men to remain silent long enough."

As a senior medical student in France in 1940, John Howard Griffin was involved in helping German and Austrian Jews escape. He sat in cheap little rooms where unspeakable human tragedy was taking place, where the parents, knowing they could go no further, pleaded with him to take their children from them, so that they might at least have the chance to live. Later he saw a similar kind of tragedy being enacted in Mississippi during the 60s.

"It seems all my life I have been sitting in rooms like that, while down in the street there were decent human people who knew nothing of what was going on in those rooms and who were even led to justify and rationalize the racism which led to the tragedy. My life has been like walking on a street toward a goal you thought you had and always finding people lying wounded in the gutter and your never being able to pass such people.

"Some of us don't want to see from the outside, but we still end up seeing from the outside. Somebody said to me that the pro-life movement was an extension of the civil rights movement. I said it was not an extension, it was identical with it. We've got to stop those committee decisions about letting a person die or stay plugged in. Now, near the end of my life, I want to make those decisions myself."

The overflow audience at the Chateau Laurier gave John Howard Griffin a prolonged standing ovation.

Communications theorist Marshall McLuhan spoke in a wholly different vein when he said that we are living in an age of loss of private identity, and at such a time it is not easy to convince people that private identity means anything. In the electronic era, tribal man has re-emerged after 2400 years. In the world of the data bank the individual becomes a statistic, he said. He cautioned his hearers they must know the kind of world they live in if they hope to change it.

Calling himself a very old man but exuding a contagious vitality, [Malcolm] Muggeridge predicted euthanasia would be the next great controversy. "I think everybody should get ready for it. It will be dressed up in humanitarian terms. The reason it has not so far made significant headway is, I believe, because everybody knows the only time it has been put into practice was under the Nazis. The argument will be twofold. First, that the patient's life, alas true, has already been practically terminated through drug sedation. Second, standards of quality of life (set by society) will require that many not measuring up should be got rid of."

Muggeridge told journalists gathered at a press conference that when "eroticism is separated from procreation" civilization is set on a downward course. In his view, contraception, abortion and euthanasia are all symptoms of the same disease. He deplored the inertia and fatalism somehow inculcated by the media on questions that lie at the heart of the western tradition.

There were many other speakers at the Festival, including Ellen McCormack, pro-life candidate for the U.S. presidency in 1976, Dick Gregory, civil rights activist and black entertainer, Phyllis Bowman, Director of the Society for Unborn Children, London, England.

* This article is based on an account of a pro-life Festival of Life on Parliament Hill attended by 3,000 people. Reprinted by permission of *B.C. Catholic*.

May 27, 1977

Dear John knee:

Weekend coming up with the Don Jail, Sharon, Pentecost Commitment – We have a new group ready to go to Metropolitan Toronto East Detention Centre – about 16. We're going to go there Monday, June 27, on a trial basis before we begin to go on a regular basis in the fall. We'll be with those who are sentenced – staying about three months. There'll be about 25 for each evening over a month. We need to renew the Vanier prison group – Rudy Stocking and I are planning to pick out some new people.

> Viktor Frankl now 1500
> Still long way to go
> But slowly unfolding
> If ever you could make it
> It'd be fantastic For you
> especially
> At this time of your life.

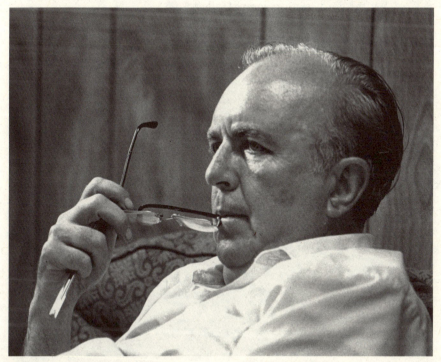

Fr. Tom in a pensive moment

Friendship and Second Innocence

Sharon now filled Five weekends
200 each Families ready to
communicate Their experience of
sharing.
May still be afraid to see doctor
Hopefully after Tuesday She'll
return again And face the reality.
Human support is significant But
the pros are necessary And one
cannot run Away from the truth.
After three days of silence I
phoned her
Found her listening again. Called
her to phone and face it. She did!
Watching the hockey game
between Quebec Nordiques
and Winnipeg even Though
the score 8–3
Is already known. Doing it
just to Keep relaxed
while writing and
flowing.

Love,

Tommy

May 31, 1977

Dear Tom,

Beyond all this my feelings about you are totally at peace. I feel you and I have reached a blessed stage of understanding, openness, oneness, that is as nearly total as two humans can ever reach. I feel absolutely secure and safe in your physical and spiritual presence, in the solid strength of our union of hearts. I hope this brings you one small percentage of the comfort and joy and peace it brings me. I hope it is truly as great a gift in your life as it is in mine.

John

P.S. I have always wondered if two people could really be truthful to one another, truly open, truly daring ... Now I know ... Thanks be to God I do know.

June 2, 1977

I got a card today from a Jesuit teacher in St. Louis with these words from Leon Bloy: Joy is the most infallible sign of the presence of God.

John

July 4, 1977 (John's journal)

For Tommy:

People have been in and out. Am not entirely sure just what has been going on. Have two big work projects – the chapter on Merton and the story and photos for Youth Corps. It is like pushing a mountain to do these things, to think, to sit up. The least little obstacle, since I can hardly walk and no one really can do things for me, seems insurmountable. I work at a snail's pace and then forget what I have already done and where I am to resume work.

I make plans, perhaps for the retreat in August. Things like that keep hope alive when my body tells me overwhelmingly that my time is short, when my body begs me to lie down and go to sleep, to give up this battle to get up and work, especially when the least work, even taking a bath or writing a letter, seems unbelievably difficult.

July 8, 1977 (John's journal)

I can hardly bear to see or speak to anyone else, except TM [Tom McKillop] and Joe Noonan – people like that. TM especially seems to be the one who knows and who is there always in the most desperate moments. He is my connection with almost everything having to do with living and life right now, with the mystery of what is happening to me. I read the Mass and that is about the only thing that connects me with a moment's light. It is very difficult to sustain thought long enough to pray, so I let what is happening do the praying. Mostly, I think it prays for the problems confronting so many priests these days – the problems of what is real and what is specious within the vocation: the problems in the modern world of being both human and living fully the priestly vocation as alter-Christs. Especially when so little help really comes from the theologians who are so intent on being not only with it, but "ahead of it," when about half of the theologizing comes from the brain and the other half from the affective needs, rationalizing them without really understanding them or living them in Jesus. Very little seems to come from that authentic human blending of heart and mind and integrity.

I do not think people shy away from the priesthood so much because of the "angelism" of the old days, utterly unrealistic as it was, as because today it represents too much the "shifting sands" of no real principles at all, other than that we be somehow "free" (which means in too many cases not a freedom based on the total gift of self to God and to God's will centring on the Jesus who inhabits within us, but relying entirely on uninstructed intuition and a kind of utterly unreal legalism that allows us to be "technically" okay, all in being totally contrary to the spirit of our vocation).

So we replace the old masks with the new ones. The old masks were frequently hateful – stern, inhuman, dehumanized, hard ... how well we remember them. The new masks? They are often wide open, swinging, ass-revealing. Somewhere in between, the sheep look for Christ and do not find him in either of these masks and end up weeping for frustration.

I have been able to listen in the night and try to be guided, never really knowing if it was His voice or my own clangour, trying to get rid of my own clangour. In any case, like so many others, I thirsted for an authentic holiness – mostly all I saw was play-acting. I have seen it in enough people to know it exists and I have had that rare privilege of seeing enough truthful, real, priests – those at least who never give up the struggle and who are authentically in love with Jesus and in love with humanity with a "Jesus" love – to give light in that gloom of mediocrity one otherwise encounters on all sides. The Abrahamic minority is much tinier than most would like to believe. Never has mankind so craved that it increase. How can those who really see ever hold back anything for themselves? This is why I love those who do see and who do give – many of the great men, some of them priests, some of them with other vocations ... it doesn't matter. I think offhand of the two TMs (Merton and McKillop); of Mother Teresa, Simon Scanlon, Jim O'Donnell and Bill O'Donnell ... so many, many who finally got free through this route.

Perhaps the most profound motive of all is the sudden realization that came to me the other night, that I am here one with you simply to remain your intimate companion – not to coach or judge you but only to be there in you sharing fully your pains and your triumphs, your moments of sadness and weakness and strengths, dissolved in each other as we are and together dissolved in Jesus, "one becoming One," as you put it once.

God love you, Tommy. May you, in your busy life, find moments to come back there into your centre from time to time and find rest and encouragement and companionship and truth – the integrity that alone can save us. May you feel the smile, the hug, the embrace, the kiss, both in moments of great fullness and in those of emptiness. When you listen in the night and hear those words that I say to you, may you hear them as coming from the love of Jesus, as I hear them when you speak them to me.

July 10, 1977 (John's journal)

I put these things down not to complain, but because I suppose there should be a record, if only for myself. I listen for the Beloved and hear no voice. This is part of this condition – waiting, waiting! I try to remember advice and none of it comes back clear. I say Yes and offer this up, but I long, I ache from the loneliness.

Only the primitive remains of life: the writer who has to write down everything in order to understand it; the lover who craves, craves to be buried in the Beloved, just to rest there and draw strength. But all of that is lost in this fog of no physical feeling in the arms or legs, no easy way to breathe. There is hunger for some pleasure, no matter how slight, to break this grip of misery.

I miss seeing my comfortable friends – all of them are gone. All of them are doing the things they ought to be doing. My deepest friend is the busiest of all, doing the most important things of all.

I am a man dead on his feet and still passionately in love. The only words that break through in their full meaning at such times are "love" and "innocence." Those two words in conjunction with each other ... innocent love that is nevertheless total. Innocence is difficult for me, as it always has been. Innocent love is the supreme love. I have tried to be obedient to it with many failures. It comes now at the end of my life, perhaps. Though I have to have the help of the love in order to remain innocent.

Let us do whatever has to be done in order to go on helping one another to become saints. That is the one thing we must never lose. I have this great passion to offer. I offer it for the innocence and the sanctity of priests who must show the way to the hungerers after the absolute; and who must stop falling into all of the traps that beset them.

I did not feel abandoned in that sense, for my friends have been more than faithful. But Tom came and took care of me as only he could have done it. He dressed my wounds, gave me my shots, bathed me, brought me the Sacraments, listened to my confessions, held me and soothed me in moments of great weakness, loved me in the deepest sense of that word; and afterwards could write: "Eleven days of holiness, nakedness, modesty, love and compassion." We were brothers, but more than brothers, because we could bare every corner of our souls, from our most abject weaknesses to our highest aspirations, with no fear of being anything but loved and helped along the whole gamut.

I once told him, "People like us can find our happiness only in innocence." That is perhaps the truest thing I ever said about myself, at least; and I feel it is equally true of him and of many another who does not really realize that. In very difficult times he has helped me to remain innocent.

July 15, 1977

Dear Tom,

It is mid-afternoon now. After writing you this morning, a short note, I began to have severe abdominal cramps and my blood pressure rose, it was pounding in my head. We called the doctor and he had Piedy bring me in immediately.

I prayed for you, blessed buddy, and wished that my miseries offered for you would be enough to help you find the peace you need, or wished I could help you some way. You have been a godsend to me in this whole matter of helping me return to some semblance of physical innocence. How I wished that if that were your problem and it was any burden to you, I could help you in the same way. I say that without intending to attach too much importance to it, or emphasizing it too much, but you know that I am here praying for your health and happiness and clarity, and if you ever need me, you must call me. It would help me so much to be able to stand or sit by your side in any difficulty.

You know the mountaintops and the valleys, the batting high and the slumps. You are a man who lives in the real and is not affronted to face the real. I know that you do not really believe it when you say, "You can't always be good." It is the truth, of course. But I don't believe that deep in your heart you feel that it has to be the truth.

I don't know what I am saying, blessed. I am as sick as a damned mule.

All I am asking is that you do not carry your personal burdens alone, old friend. I share all of mine with you and it is such a godsend of a help. Let me at least help you carry any of yours that could be helped by sharing them with me. I know you do that a great deal. You should never hesitate to do it fully. Surely you will feel no more humiliation in putting them in my heart than I have felt putting mine in your heart.

I expect a great deal of your fatigue comes not only from the reality of so many people's problems, but also from the sheer fatigue of battling constantly against the shallowness, falsity and delusions that complicate those real problems.

I have always found I could come out of more by diverting my attention from it than by fruitlessly trying to battle it through.

A note from Joe Noonan, full of wit and useless information which always delights me; he tells me in this one that in a 1601 edition of the Bible, this commandment appeared exactly this way: "Thou shalt commit adultery."

He remarks that that must be the most catastrophic typesetting error in the history of printing.

John

July 16, 1977 – Feast of Our Lady of Mount Carmel

Dear Tom,

Well, I won't give in to them today. I cannot. I have your handkerchief, a great deterrent, and the candle, and sometime before evening I will find the concentration to say the prayers and to read through the Mass for Our Lady of Mount Carmel, who has been such a special protectress to me for so many years, but who, in my present physical weakness, seems distant indeed.

I have just finally got through reading today's Mass. These words of the Gospel came alive, as though Jesus were saying them of Big T:

> Here is my servant whom I have chosen, my beloved, the favourite of my soul, and I will endow him with my spirit and he will proclaim the true faith to the nations. He will not brawl or shout, nor will anyone hear his voice in the streets.

> He will not break the crushed reed nor put out the smouldering wick till he has led the truth to victory ...

I once thought some of those words were meant for me. I took them to heart, which is why I always worked so quietly, so secretly. Or at least sincerely tried to.

Sometimes, I think that in spite of all my deficiencies and weaknesses Jesus must have loved me very much at times, to send me the great gift of a brother, a twin of the soul and perhaps even a twin of the body, to provide the strengths there where I have none left.

You said once that had we become close many years earlier, you would probably have got into all sorts of trouble. No, I would never have led you into that kind of trouble; we would both have got in trouble for raising so much hell about injustice.

John

July 17, 1977

Dear Old Tommy,

You are at the big double-header game today and that makes me happy. I hope it is a good game and that you do not yell yourself hoarse – or perhaps that you do. I have never been to a ball game, but I think of it as great excitement, popcorn, soft drinks on a hot day, hot dogs and things like that, all of which fill my affections.

Shortly after I talked with you this morning, I had a good conversation with Fr. Tarcy and Brother Patrick Hart at Gethsemani. They were calling me about a point of argument in Merton's life, which I could settle for them quite easily, and then we talked a long time. It was good to hear from such friends.

Then I printed up the enclosed photo of Fr. Thompson's parents, made when they came to see me a week or so ago. This picture is kind of like the locusts the other day – it brings back those early days that now seem so incredible, when we were going through hell together in Louisiana. Such people these are. Their son is a priest and a splendid one and yet he was not even allowed to say Mass in his own parish church after his ordination. They never lost their faith. They were fully there in heart when their son had to hide me out again and again when I was being pursued by the Ku Klux Klan in Mississippi and Louisiana. He was always outspoken and unbelievably courageous and it is a miracle that he was not exterminated. Just seeing this photo of me with these gentle but brave and strong people who slaved to give all their children educations (though the father, Louis, cannot read or write), holding onto each others' hands while the father holds to mine, moves me tremendously. They came all the way from Houston in the heat "to see a sick friend." Their presence here was like a blessing on the house, the way it is when you are here. I think of all the world's great and famous and honoured people who have visited me here and I think of none (except you) who brought more ease and light and love than these beautiful people. Like you, they know the "other side" of me (symbolically): they know me as the black man who stood by their son and who said to the bishops and the world the very things they were aching to say but could not (because no one would listen). They know me as a brother, the way you do (though of course in a far different way). I hope someday you get to meet these wonderful souls who have been tested by fire and humiliation ever since they were born. Because you have the same kind of simplicity, they would love you as you would love them. How irresistible is their kind of goodness and yours. How much I am nourished by them, as by you ... more so than by all of those who wear the masks of perfection.

Mandy adores Fr. August. He has known her since she was born, of course and they were always great pals. Mandy asked me, in an off-handed way, if she could have as much fun with you as she did with him. I told her that you were more timid, but that if she ever opened up, she would find you the finest kind of friend.

Friendship and Second Innocence

From left: Mr. Thompson, Mrs. Thompson, John Howard Griffin, Fr. August Thompson, and Piedy Griffin

Although Fr. August and I have never been as close as you and I – as interiorily united and harmonious – we have been through all the hells of hiding, bombings, great fear, etc., together. He is pure gold, able to function superbly even in great fear. I never saw him break but once and that was privately with me when he knew he was to be bombed by the KKK and the bishop would not even order him out of town for that weekend. That was the weekend I found the money to get him to Atlanta (because he didn't have a penny); and that was the night three bombs were found under his bedroom window. Those were times when unheroic people were simply called out of themselves, called on to be heroic. I had begged the bishop to send him away for just that one weekend and he had said all he could do was "pray" for Fr. August.

I think the thing that binds us the closest, Tom, is some connection at this level. You have a profound awareness of this kind of cauldron beneath the surface of life today. You see it in the problems of young and old. You are aware that it is a time when some have to do something to try to penetrate the covering gloss that barely hides our dehumanization. You are no more one of those muscle-bound feelingless heroes than any of the rest of us. You are hurt by the disesteem of others, you are disgusted by the meaningless values you so often encounter among your brothers who have no view of what is happening. You feel the deep urgency to obey the will of God, all in being a lonely human being. This is why our friendship is so precious to me. Like me, you will always be surrounded by people who pat you on the back while pissing in your pocket, so that even "honours" come to be meaningless, because honours never come until it is safe for the establishment to give its nod of approval, and the establishment never catches on while the danger is present – or even while the need is present. It is only when they think you are "harmless" that the honours come, as a kind of cowardly cop-out that gives the establishment the illusion they were right there fighting the good battle all the time. How rare in this kind of life is the companionship that sticks firm and stays supportive and loves the whole person.

It touches me that you have fears and do not sleep very well alone in the house; it touches me that after giving all to the mountaintop, emptying yourself of everything for the good of the kingdom, being Tom McKillop, the giant capable of creating Youth Corps and Sharon Corps and all the rest and touching the hearts of thousands and exhausting yourself in the process, you then have some time alone and face the inner reality of very basic and very human physical needs and do a triple header there in your loneliness. You got only three Hail Marys. I expect if Jesus himself were giving out the penance, you would have got none, considering all the circumstances.

Since it is a matter of physical and nervous release without images, it is a much less serious matter than Brother Locust's. Now, you have to help me become Brother Eagle, at least in my imagination, since I am not physically capable of a great deal of "majestic soaring," old buddy. Well, Brother Ass-head is probable the most fitting of all.

All for the moment. Time for me to go get the "deep shot," the one that is so difficult for Piedy to give and for me to receive.

God love you, baby.

Love,

Johnny

July 18, 1977 – 26th Anniversary of my First Communion

Dear Tom,

I love this Gospel – "Come to me, all of you who labour and are overburdened, and I will give you rest ... and you will find rest for your souls. Yes, my yoke is easy and my burden light." That last line always mystifies me, because I never found his yoke easy or his burden light – which comes I suppose from the fact that I have always been weaker than most, and what is easier for the strong ones has always been a labour and a sweat for me ... though of course it has also always been the only possible way for me because all the other ways ended up in dead ends.

I have just read tomorrow's Mass, the feast of St. Bonaventure. He and Aquinas were great friends. They met in Paris when both stayed at the Convent St. Jacques and walked each evening in conversation in the little weed-filled courtyard. One of my greatest things when I was losing my sight and studying there was to walk in those footsteps in that same circular path among the weeds, thinking about their conversations, sometimes conversing myself with Fr. Marie-Bruno about their conversations – in my early formation when I understood only fragments (as I still do).

John

✶ ✶

July 26, 1977

Dear Tom,

And also in answer to a letter from someone bitching about time wasted in contemplation, Merton answered,

> However, the greatest joy does not come from the quiet, the peace it produces in a man's heart, but in awakening and attuning the heart to the voice of Jesus, to the inexplicable, quick definite inner certitude of one's call to obey Him, to hear Him, to worship Him there in the silence, alone; and that is the whole reason for one's existence; because this makes all our existence and actions fruitful and gives fruitfulness to all one's contacts and is the ransom and purification of one's heart that has been dead in sin.

Aren't those profoundly beautiful lines?

The only other person with whom I have felt as deep a sharing was the person of Jesus (I mean you are the only one who comes so close to that and of course you are closer, because we are two humans). I have never hidden a speck of myself – body, mind or soul – from Jesus. I have never hidden a speck of myself – body, mind or soul – from you. I have always felt obliged to hide portions of my reality from all other people who have entered or passed through my life ... if for nothing else just to spare them the harsher realities of my badness, but mostly because of my training in the fact that some things "have to be kept secret" – the same training you have had and that so many of us have had. I am forever grateful that at the human level we have at least broken through that with one another. It is an immense help in keeping us both anchored in our realities.

John

July 27, 1977

Dear Tom,

Now that we can't be together as much by phone, let's try to be together as much in our thoughts and spirit as possible. Each morning I remember you at the morning Office especially; and also at noon; and also at Mass, with a kiss of peace in spirit and of course many times during the day in addition to those special times.

John

Monastery of the Maximinims of Milpitis

"As the ego diminishes, the Maximinim learns that Nothing is really something."—Anonymous

July 28, 1977

Advise me, Brethren,

For I know not what to do. Being on retreat at the Maximinim mother house in Milpitas, I have found the very foundations of the place shaken. Next door, on the property between our haven and the waste-water treatment plant, the Milpitians have erected a Praise-God-A-Drome. The Milpitians are an order of the very most modern charismatic monks. Their Praise-God-A-Drome, according to Abbot Babbit, is "an Astrodome of the Spirit, acres of enclosed space for thousands of public conversations with the Holy Spirit." Unfortunately, neighbors cannot help eavesdropping.

Sixty-five thousand glossolaliacs do not make a Maximinimal noise. Particularly when they are responding to – "Give me a 'G': give me an 'o': give me a 'd'." The vibrations unleashed by the masses or half-massed charismatics are not good vibes: the foundations of our mother house have developed several cracks thanks to earth tremors.

When I tried to explain to Abbot Babbit that Maximinims need peace and quiet in which to minimize, that open-faced sandwich of a man declared that the Holy Spirit wishes us to maximize our potential for interpersonal relationships, to abandon the vices of the solitary (he explained that he was referring to contemplation) and to get with the It which so many have found. The Abbot insisted that he was not making mere personal recommendations but real Third Person-al recommendations.

So, my problem is this: if I seek an injunction against noise pollution, will the Maximinims appear to be abating the Spirit? Please share your opinions on this matter. My quandary is interfering with minimization. I had a distinct urge to increase just a few minutes ago.

H E L P !

Brother Infinitesimo

Big T – just to keep you informed about the problems of our order.

Less is Human: to be least, divine! — Maximinims of Milpitas

✶ ✶

July 28, 1977

Dear Tom,

I cannot bear, as you know, to see anyone unhappy or in grief, though I know those are human and valuable emotions. They just shred me.

John

July 30, 1977

Dear Tom,

Prayed for you – that you are under less tension now; that you had a good visit with Jim; that Jesus would watch over you day and night and that this deepest of friendships would give you some rest and joy.

I tell you the truth: the only person who does not seem to fragment any of this by presence or voice is you. I suppose because you are the only one before whom I can feel as free as I have felt in solitude only in the presence of Jesus.

In this oneness, I have felt that my falls have in a sense been a betrayal not only of myself, but in a sense of you. The world needs all the generosity and sacrifice people like us can muster. That became clear once again (for the millionth time) in my prayers last night. Perhaps one extra prayer, one deeper loving sacrifice can make the difference. I always feel this in any case, which is one of the reasons why I am so devastated when I fail – I have somehow deprived someone of a possible grace. That is why I feel an almost childlike gratitude to you for the times when you have stopped me, when you have brought me out of these self-fevers.

John

* *

July 31, 1977

Dear John,

Tom McKillop and John Howard Griffin at St. Michael's College, University of Toronto

We've decided to ask Ivan Burgess to sing before you at Massey Hall and Convocation Hall. He was delighted. He is the black singer who did it in 1968. He's a beautiful person, just finished a sabbatical of creativity, drama, music, poetry and writing plays. He sings Caribbean, French, Eastern Canada, American material and his own compositions. I talked with him of the possibility of Luiz doing a spectacular at the end of the afternoon at Massey Hall and at the end of the evening at Convocation Hall. To have him on first might be heavy for the youth at the beginning, but near the end he will lift their hearts and bodies. Ivan liked the idea of even the visibility dimension of a Canadian Bermudian, a BIG TEXAN and a Brazilian American. Wonder if Luiz would do it – a couple of numbers appropriate for the occasion.

The reason why I called the topic "Racism: Blindness or Vision" was that I hoped you might speak of your personal blindness experience and use it in an analogical way to describe racism and vision, to be an analogous expression of love, brotherhood, community. What do you think? I mention this because when the principal in charge of principals asked me about the possible content, I gave some of your background and this seemed to be an interesting way of helping the students to grasp the insight of racism.

Gordon Cressey sent along further material for your talk with the principals on multi-cultural programs in the schools. It might give you an insight into some of the attempts. He personally is very committed to leading the schools towards social justice.

Everything is happening in a beautiful, flowing way. The bishop agreed to let me live alone for one year – the parishes are beginning to become one-man parishes. This could be a good experience. I just need to move the body early in the morning to begin with a longer session of prayer.

The team is going great. We've gone to nine zones of priests to introduce them to our work with youth.

At the leadership day at Sharon on Sunday we moved people towards the Griffin Seminar. Who? John Howard Griffin? Who's that? Oh yes, I read that! He's dead, isn't he?

"The Lord gives and almost took away."

Enclosed is the booklet that we hope will motivate the youth and their leaders on a journey.

Had dinner with Gerry and David Graham (young poet) the other evening and then went over to hear James Douglas and his wife Shelley speak of the Pacific Life Community and their civil disobedience regarding the Trident (I.C.B.M.) in Washington State. His book *Resistance and Contemplation* gripped me deeply. I questioned him openly on Jesus. He was very vague – seemed hurt by theology or seems to be reacting to mist around the image of Jesus, though he and she are within the Christian tradition.

The minister at the meeting felt that I was putting down a good meeting – I really was calling them forth to say the root or source. They didn't and I was disappointed! They've called one of their boys Tom Merton. He is on his way to Washington to protest Trident. Sr. Mary Alban may go with him and a few others.

Fr. Tom standing in front of the Sharon Corps Vision Statement banner

All the best from here.

Sincerely in Jesus,

Tom McKillop

✲ ✲

August 1, 1977

Dear Tom,

Two prominent people in Fort Worth with heart conditions that dragged along committed suicide this weekend. (Saturday afternoons and Sundays seem particularly difficult at such times.) I keep trying to avoid that starkness, keep saying yes, keep offering it up for whatever good it can do. I know this is the right, the only thing to do. I am not sure this would continue to be bearable without our blessed friendship, which shines through the darkness when almost nothing else will.

I do not think the new "openness" means exposing oneself in intimate matters to the whole damned world – it cheapens everything. Such matters should be shared only with the closest of friends. Then such sharing can be a blessed help and a true blessing. Otherwise, no.

John

✶✶

August 2, 1977

Dear Tom,

In this union of spirit, I ask myself so many times a day, "Where is Tom now? What is he doing?" And those questions are prayers for you wherever you are and in whatever you are doing. The prayer is always for your happiness and fulfillment wherever you might be. I think of Cassian's statement, "The only real prayer comes when we are unaware that we are praying." I do not exactly believe that. I believe that conscious prayer is also prayer, but that it probably leads us into those depths of unconscious prayer in which we are simply always aware of the presence of Jesus, sitting there like a friend, sharing in whatever we do or think, loving us and being loved in return, even in our busiest activities. Since He sent you to indwell there in those same places at the centre of my being, there is in me always a sense of your being, your presence, your loving and being loved in return.

I told Him that if He really longed for a true relationship, it would happen and it would seem almost to happen by accident as His life naturally crossed the lives of others; that coming to love another profoundly was not something that could be forced or even deliberately planned.

John

✶✶

August 4, 1977 (John's journal)

God help me to think of the feelings of others. God help me to put others where they really are – first and before myself. Pray that I not be drawn into this awful shrivelling of the heart.

John

September 7, 1977

After talking with you, old Tom, I managed to do a little work on the Merton – the first I have managed (and it was poor) in a long time. Anyway, it was good to do anything except lie here on this bed.

John

September 9, 1977

These times are like sensible graces, washing everything clean, giving light. No sleep again last night, but the sleeplessness was peace-filled, love-filled, commitment-filled, without the sense of misery that so often comes. This morning the right hand is still ice, the pulse still 44. I have a call in to the doctor.

September 16, 1977

Dear Tom,

Relapse this afternoon. How I wanted to call you at Sharon, but it seemed overwhelmingly complicated. Complete interior desolation. Unable to move or go to supper. Better tonight: why? Susie wanted a banana shake – the first I've made since you left. I offered to make it as it did when I made them for you.

John

September 20, 1977

Dear Tom,

Much of the wakeful times, when everything came up in gagging and vomiting, I found some contentment in thinking about the treasure of our friendship, my immense identification with you in your work; in your human needs; in the good movements that we have known together and still know together; in your priesthood; in my love for you, which is inseparable from my love for Jesus; in my gratitude that I can communicate with you and get answers even when it seems I hear only the silence of Jesus.

John

September 22, 1977

Dear Tom,

Now I have thought of a *B – IN – GO* for you, old blessed:

Be yourself; be – have, be well in mind, soul, body and (your expression) at least a little holy; more if possible, than just a little.

IN and open to all grace; in – spired; in truth, in vigour and happiness, in ease of conscience.

GO in good sense, in fidelity, in the charity of Jesus, in rest enough to have zest.

And may all your *BINGO*s carry the three messages instead of the one explosive one.

That is lousy poetry, blessed, but I am no Thomas à Buckett.

I pray with all my heart as I become more and more deprived of the physical functioning that attaches us to life and happiness. I beg God to make my friends that much more involved in life, that much more appreciative of everything good about living and that much happier. I hope you think of that when you get up in the morning and are free to go take a bath, to walk up and down the stairs of your blessed home without ever thinking about it, when you hear the sounds of the train in the night; when you, after a tiring session at the office, can get up and walk around the block to clear your mind and restore your energies. I am not saying what you have and what I no longer have, baby – you know that. It is not a complaint – it is just that you should relish those things and I hope you do.

John

September 24, 1977

I attach myself to a cherished daydream – that of living far out in the country, away from everything, in a cabin, a small, clean room, with a fenced-in chicken yard just outside. Able to do simple things that take the time healthily, in feeding the chickens, baking the bread ... it is a cheerful scene, a life reduced to essentials, as mine now is, but in a setting far different ... far from the specious activity of cities and their noises and the cruelties that are inevitable when so many people have to struggle, mostly against each other, to make it. Well, it is only a daydream. 6:30 – Activity in the house. Johnny is here, listening to the football game. Piedy and Susie are cooking supper. Steve has gone to pick up my mother. They are thinking about playing cards, hoping I will get interested. There is no way I can play cards, but the atmosphere is cheerful, anyway.

John

September 24, 1977

Trying to read last evening, as an alternative to calling you or falling to pieces, I read of the tremendous friendship of Tennyson and Hallam, so like ours, and these lines written by Tennyson after Hallam's death: "My love involves the love before, / My love is how, / Passion thou / Though mixed with God and Nature vaster / I seem to love thee more and more." May such be true of us. May I be kept alive in your faithful heart long after everyone else forgets.

John

One of Many Gourmet Recipes Used by John Howard Griffin

Pain au lait

1 cup milk
1 tbsp. sugar
5 tbsp. sweet butter
2 tsp. salt
1 cup lukewarm water
1 package dry yeast
5 1/2 cups sifted all purpose flour
4-5 tbsp. melted butter, cooled (for brushing dough)
1 egg, beaten

1) Put milk, sugar, salt, butter in a pan. Stir over moderate heat until mixture comes to boil. Cool the mixture to lukewarm.

2) Put lukewarm water in large bowl. Sprinkle yeast over it, stir with wooden spoon or pastry hook until it dissolves.

3) Combine liquids.

4) Stir in 3 cups sifted flour gradually. Mix well.

5) Stir in remaining 2 1/2 cups flour.

6) Flour kneading board. Turn out dough and knead thoroughly, about ten minutes, until it is smooth.

7) Form dough into ball. Place in lightly floured container for rising. Brush top surface thoroughly with melted, cooled butter. Cover bowl with plastic wrap and a warm cloth.

8) Let rise 1 hour 20 minutes in warm place.

9) Knock down – do not knead again. Turn out onto floured board.

10) Preheat oven to 375°F.

11) Butter one large or two smaller loaf pans. Shape dough and put in pans. Slash. Brush with egg.

12) Put dough in warm place and let dough rise until nearly double (about 15 minutes). Keep dough covered with cloth supported by drinking glasses – cloth should not touch dough.

13) Set pans on jelly roll sheet or baking sheet and bake 45 minutes.

14) Reduce heat to 350°F and bake another 20 minutes or until done.

Cool on wire rack after removing from pan.

September 25, 1977

Dear Tom,

Now, at 3:00, I read through the texts of today's Mass. I unite myself in spirit to the 4:00 Mass in Scarboro.

It occurs to me again how stupid is most of the speculation about dying, something indulged in only by the living. The dying do not speculate – they just do it, and mostly in struggle and bewilderment, hungering for a happy moment here, a loving moment there. All of the truly stratospheric music, those expressions of great eternal and transcendent beauty, are not bearable to me anymore – not because of the hearing problems, but because the slow movement from the Opus 132 quartet of Beethoven, for example, or the Mozart G minor quintet, simply hurt too deeply. They make you face things you are already too near to facing. A profound instinct to struggle even when no strength remains, to go on struggling; you get up and fall back. You sit up and type even though thoughts are too difficult to express and the typing is too difficult to do; you keep on even when you can't keep on.

Later. Dusk. 97 degrees outside. Supper a good marrow bone – two, in fact; a little roast okra.

John

September 27, 1977

It has also been a year of learning about weakness – physical, moral, spiritual – and losing that clutter of illusions about any strength in any of those areas. Those are illusions on which we build our lives as men. In the long testing, they vanish and you learn to count on nothing but mercy, and once they are all gone, and soul, mind, body are stripped of them, then mercy comes in abundance, though it is often difficult to perceive except in the actions of friends. A new kind of truth, as bare as your weakness, comes in the voices of friends, and in their actions, in things that surface and that you are allowed to glimpse – as Sharon; as the little community dedicating themselves to the most miserable in the ghetto of Cleveland; as Trevor's work in Philadelphia and Simon's in San Francisco and God knows how many others. These are individuals seeking to humanize at the level of individuals the utter inhumanity of the "system" that is heartless in its inefficacious worship of efficacity.

John

September 29, 1977

Dear Tom,

I hope and pray that my going through it as decently as possible may lead God to space such deaths to those you and I love. Since my ardent hope is that God will spare you such an ending, I tell you about it as much as I can, so you will understand what such a friendship means to a man like me and why I view it as such a precious gift. It is as though God means to allow me to taste fully the stripping, to lift me up from the place at the foot of the cross and put me on it, but to make it more bearable for a weakling like me by sending a Christ-filled son who is as human as I am. I had always secretly thought I would die a martyr and prepared for that and offered it if God wanted it. Some saint described martyrdom as "a brief agony and an eternity of paradise." God chose differently, but he sent me a brother to help keep me faithful, to be the Beloved-filled beloved. All of that is involved in the precious gift. God gave far more than He is taking away, as He always will if we really try to give everything of ourselves to Him. The fact that He would do this for such a poor specimen as I am proves the generosity.

Later: 2:35 your time. I judge you are finishing the Mass about now. I prayed a special intention: that if this struggling, tired heart has to go on beating itself out in a slower death, it could feel the peace and strength of being supplemented, carried, supported by the love of your strong heart and nourished by your thoughts and prayers; and that my virtually incessant prayers for your intentions, whatever they may be, keep a reservoir of peace in you despite the fragmentations and frustrations of a human life given in Jesus' work for others.

I say yes ... and at least, hope, hope, hope that the resonances of all this go out somewhere and help someone, and that you and I go on sharing the dream in union with one another, even more unified when I am physically dead than now, if that is possible.

John

✶ ✶

September 30, 1977

Dear John,

> Read reflections
> you miss Nothing
> almost In descriptions
> Even while Unconscious
> and blind You grasp
> The essence Of faces
> Expressions, crisis
> Whose missing? And
> never
> Forget elephant-style
> Tonight we Do a series
> Of experiences With
> youth At St. Barnabas
> On Life
> Demands and
> Response. Music,
> film Paula, Sil
> Discussions, groups
> Curiosity questions
> Mystery searchings
> Sharings, planning
> For future Ahead.
> Need of support Challenge,
> encouragement. Saturday
> Maplehurst Theme of
> New Beginnings. An
> interview In the
> morning With
> young adult

Friendship and Second Innocence

    Inspirational. Sunday Vanier
    Theme your
    Favourite one
    Life after Life
    Bottom of well
    Experience.
    Woman or man At
    prison
    Having Eucharist
    At night
    Mystery questions
    Again, again
    Hoping for Great
    night.

Love and Peace,

Tommy

✶ ✶

October 2, 1977

Dear Tom,

Just went through the 4:00 p.m. Mass with you at Sharon, from memory, though I did not have the texts and of course did not hear the homily. I concentrated on the intentions of everyone there and said a deep prayer for your own intentions and in union with them, as I did this morning when they brought me Communion. Thank you for calling me from Sharon last night, old buddy.

Note on material for Merton:

St. Francis de Sales – "There is no harm done to saints if their faults are shown as well as their virtues. But great harm is done to everybody by those hagiographers who slur over the faults, be it for the purpose of honouring the saints, or through fear of diminishing our reverence for their holiness. These writers commit a wrong against the saints and against the whole of posterity."

John

✶ ✶

October 10, 1977

Dear Tom,

Other phone calls – Fr. Stan ... Studs Turkel ... Viktor Frankl called this morning from Vienna – a very beautiful conversation. He had received your letter. He called to tell me that he and Elly were carrying me in love every day. "But in a real way," he said, "your greatness in handling this situation is a broadening thing for your friends, but also a burden, because I, for one, know that I could not be so great in handling it – few men could. But you show us the way."

Elly Frankl, John Howard Griffin and Viktor Frankl.
Credit: Tom McKillop

I felt like dying of embarrassment, Tommy. Knowing me, you know why. But he was talking about how I ought to be rather than how I am, and that helps me to want, at least, to become that way. It was like hearing from you ... a conversation from heart to heart, utterly open and without pretense and without the kind of specious dishonesty of so many conversations.

When I sometimes ask you to hold on to me, to hold me in life, it comes from that. There is not an ounce of strength or bravery in me – there never was ... that is why I cling to the hope that you will be the one to deliver me gently into eternity.

October 10 (John's journal)

I think of Reverdy's statement in one of his letters to me, in which he said that people no longer believed in God and he could not worship people. How many do I know who have fallen in love with the image of what it would be to be a holy man and who act according to that image rather than out of any love for God. Their virtue, no matter how ardent, springs from a passion for themselves rather than a passion for God. That is why they all act alike, whereas the person truly "given" to the love of God, in Merton's words, is never going to fit anyone else's mystique.

October 11, 1977 (John's journal)

"For God's sake," I protested, "I don't teach anybody to be like me; if you must teach them anything, teach them to become truly themselves."

Things got very painful last evening. I went into another of those strange drowses, where I can hear things and know distantly what is happening, but feel out of it, near sleep. The family is quite marvellous at such times. Piedy gave me a nitroglycerine. She went and got my mother to come and spend the night. Around midnight, when I got up to go to the bathroom, I noticed the reading light was on in my mother's room. She asked me if everything was all right. I told her it was better and sat down in the chair near her bed. In the small circle of the bedlamp, her wrinkles and her age were accented and I thought she was very beautiful. She talked easily. She was reading *The Art of Southern Cooking*, obviously unable to sleep because of her anxiety over me. We talked about the book. She read me a number of recipes to see if I thought she could make such things without too much trouble. It was a beautiful, easy hour, made easier a little earlier by a call from Fr. Tom. No attack last night. Slept fairly peaceably once I got to sleep.

October 13, 1977 (John's journal)

Tomorrow, the great feast of one of my most beloved saints, Teresa of Avila: that woman of such marvellous insights and such healthy common sense who spent three years persevering, waiting, believing, in an absolute dark night of the soul, loving God without getting the slightest sign that He loved her in return, until finally the great flood of love from Jesus suddenly came to her!

October 18, 1977

Dear Tom,

When such weakness pervades every cell of the body, it seems also to pervade the soul, leaving no strength to do anything, except the strength that now comes to me through love for the state of grace and dread to lose that; as though to lose it would be to turn off the last light, blow out the last candle. Writing you is a way of escaping the total darkness, of sinking out of sight, putting out the light. It is exactly noon (your time) now. Are you there? At least I imagine you are and that you are saying, "It's all right. I have you now in spirit and in prayer. You're here where it is safe in this spiritual embrace."

If Jesus died for our sins, then cannot I suffer to relive the sufferings of others? That is why I feel such a sense of failure on mornings like this, when there is so much distress and I handle it so poorly, coming to you because I cannot handle it alone, asking you to carry me, because although I can carry others, I cannot carry myself. In this state, I know a great deal about the satanic power of temptations against life, against the light. Who can battle them without help – without the graces that we never possess (or at least I feel I do not) except through the generosity of those who pray for us and stand behind us when we cannot do these things for ourselves?

If our vocation is marriage and we have no true union except sexual, then it is impure, because it is not truly union with the beloved, but only gratification, a self-centred skill. If we have a vocation other than marriage and it is truly love, then the same signs of affection do not lead and cannot lead to sexual union because such would be not love but selfishness. But the union with the beloved person can be total and full of affection that is in no way unfree because it cannot be selfish. In or out of marriage we can and do sin in these ways, but we never can cause sin in the beloved. We cannot be impure in love. We mistake love for something else when we seek the impure union (within or outside marriage) with the beloved.

Once that is authentic we are free to love and to act, because we cannot harm the truly beloved. This is the deepest union of love that seeks union with the beloved. This is truly the "integrated" life, whether in the innocence of marriage or the innocence of celibacy. You cannot harm the beloved by leading the beloved into sin or impurity. You cannot even think that "our love makes it beautiful and all right." Then it is not love! It is something else. It is only a fragment of love that seems beautiful at the moment but will leave the taste of sin in both bodies and souls and hearts eventually. Eventually, you will have harmed the beloved and the Beloved. The one becoming one can then never really become One. The one becoming one ends up being one becoming two fragments.

John

✶ ✶

October 19, 1977 – St. Isaac Jogues

Dear Tom,

This is a day so filled with pain I do not know how to endure it any longer. I hope I can talk with you tonight. I tried most of last night when I had to sit up in the chair. I guessed that you spent the night with friends and tried to call, only to find the line busy, because I got some late calls from my nephew and my brother in Venezuela – and the phone was tied up forever.

Said Mass with you at 3:45 p.m. today, but the only words that penetrated were those of the Communion Antiphon: "Live in Me and let Me live in you, says the Lord; he who lives in Me and I in him will bear much fruit ..." Cling to that in this horror, blessed brother, and offer everything, for "the labourers who are few ..." but with little grace and incessant inner weakness. Hold me ... I know I can somehow do better than this.

John

✶ ✶

October 23, 1977 (John's journal)

Last night it was Fr. Tom who called during the worst of the seizures around midnight. It was a good thing he did because he knows all the emergency procedures and I was sitting there on the side of my bed sticking nitros under the tongue, not wanting to ring the buzzer for help because my mother was over and she tends to get too deeply anxious when she sees me like this. I forget to breathe. The first thing Fr. Tom did was to get me to breathe and then he talked quietly for a while as I struggled, calming me down, anchoring me and then he just stayed on the phone quietly until the worst of the attack passed. In this kind of extreme situation, everything fades right out of sight and the most unmasked temptations assault you – the temptation not to take the medication and let the attack go ahead and take you, the temptation that tells you that everyone would be better off now without you and it would be a mercy to go ahead and die. But with these temptations comes also the realization that they are the purest evil and you continue to say "No ... no ..." and try to shake them out of your mind and the awful certainty that you should go to confession.

Often I dream of going to a quiet place like Sharon, into a great solitude where I could have help within reach if absolutely necessary; I might have a chance. Of what? Finding myself. Setting some bearings once again.

P.S. I do not believe, blessed, that my "coaching" of you, as you requested, has ever been tinged by my feelings about myself. My fear for you has been that you would unknowingly commit an injustice against yourself and the other – and this kind of thing leads to tremendous unhappiness later – and sometimes it is an irrevocable trap.

I believe you have solved both this and your personal problem as well as they can possibly be solved under the circumstances. I cannot tell you enough what a lesson it has been for me, and how much I love you for it. In view of that, then your occasional "difficulties" seem minor indeed and are perhaps a blessing in disguise.

October 24, 1977

Dear Tom,

Days of anniversary. Do you remember? A year ago today I was in Toronto, preparing to begin my Merton series for you. I had come earlier and done the TV show; you had driven me to London, Ontario, and remained there with me, then put me on the train for Windsor, where I lectured Sunday afternoon with Catherine Doherty, returned to Toronto with priest from the Scarborough Foreign Missions, staying on Wellesley Street. Monday night we had the Mass there and the Don Jail group. That week was the beginning of the opening-up, as you took me to my room and sat in a chair and I in my wheelchair and we began to pray together each evening. For the first time I was able to pray outside myself, actually uttering spontaneous prayers with you – the beginning really, after a long preparation of friendship, of a whole new and beautiful blessing of work and companionship. Included later during that time in my past confession to you, the gradual baring of heart and soul in the deep safety of a Christ-love.

John

October 27, 1977

Dear Tom,

Slept awhile and woke up choking, unable to breathe. Be with me every moment in heart, Tommy. With this kind of weakness and instability of heartbeat, I do not see how I can fail to be near the final days, though I believe it will all go slowly. Each seizure like this could go into death, and yet I come out of it and feel I have some more time. But I am weaker and weaker except for occasional spurts of energy. Today, I thought I would be able to bathe, but there is not that kind of strength.

John

October 30, 1977

Dear Tom,

You are, I hope, having a good, relaxing time with Bill and Denise and the young people. I enclose a couple of things you might be interested in. I feel sane and stable this evening, though I am passing blood in both urine and stool. God knows what the urine blood signifies. Will talk to the doctor about it tomorrow.

All for the moment, beloved brother. Next week is a big week with All Saints, All Souls and St. Martin de Porres, my special patron. May he watch over you, too.

John

October 31, 1977

Dear John,

    Love is tender
    Gesture, light and deep,

Love is fragrant
Breath, joyful and radiant
Love is sunlight
Brilliant, glowing and burning
Love is moonlight Shining, cold
and entrancing Love is the age
Transparent, coloured and glistening.
Love is the lip
Pursed, throbbing and open
Love is the person
Unfolding, expanding and present.
The papers are within
Looking forward to your book.
Praying and carrying you every day.

Sincerely in Jesus,

Tom

November 1, 1977

Dear Tom,

This was Merton's great intention – his determination not to fall into the trap of a kind of sanity of consensus, which is really an escape from the loneliness of our individual normalcy into the "averageness" of comfortable mediocrity. Merton was determined not to do this, not to live incognito to himself. For him the solution was (since he felt these things intuitively rather than understood them) to move into deeper contemplation and solitude; only alone, he felt, could he get away from that "codification of sanity" into his own freedom and truth, into harmony with reality that would allow the needs to conform to that incognito existence to vanish – regardless of the tremendous risks, spiritual and psychological.

You are not average, but you are about as "normal" as anyone I know. Very often these very "healthy neurosis" are blessings in disguise, giving us the tension we need in order to function as ourselves and should not be tampered with. Aquinas realized this in making his contradistinction between being merely average and being truly normal. I have always contended that a true and authentic psychiatrically adjusted personality was the exact equivalent of what in religion we call a saint – not a part of the anonymous mass, the codified sanity.

John

November 1, 1977 – Feast of All Saints (John's journal)

I recall in the '60s when all I heard on university campuses (from faculty) was the aimlessness and worthlessness of students who came for the fun of it. Yet those same students, so seriously underchallenged, often became heroic in their work in Mississippi. All they needed, really, was an outlet worthy of their sacrifice. Anyone who realizes and does something about it is a hero to me. Of course, many played out, but nearly all of them look back on those years as perhaps the richest of their lives. For once they did not "play it safe." Part of the tragedy of this frustration in today's young people springs from the scandals of hero figures, government leaders, religious leaders. Each one deepens the cynicism of the young until finally we view all as potential phonies. What a tremendous responsibility is assumed by those who help the young find meaning in their lives, on to this sort of self-transcendence for the good of others (and ultimately for the good of the young themselves). They then demonstrate that they have capacity for this kind of leadership, but no ability to self-transcend – even to the point of being unwilling to sacrifice for the sake of the very young they have inspired.

John

November 2, 1977

Dear Tom,

The event I guardedly mention in the enclosed notes occurred sometime early this morning. I could not sleep – could scarcely breathe lying here in the darkness, then sitting up on the side of the bed. Suddenly, unbidden, I was filled and surrounded by the unmistakable presence of Jesus. This was not in sleep. I was perfectly conscious and so overwhelmed with relief that I did not want to sleep. I believe, since it lingers on this day, that I have been through the long, dark night and that last night marked the end of it.

The experience seemed ordinary and it was familiar from the past. For literally 25 years that has been the only thing that guided me, sustained me. A year ago it disappeared. I was almost certain I was passing through the dark night, aching with loneliness during presence – but with such a devastating illness, I did not know for sure. I was not embraced, not kissed. It was something just as real but different – as though Jesus had come back and made his presence known both in my heart and in a kind of permeation in this room, overwhelming me with love. I believe now what I have long suspected: that in order to make the dark night bearable for me, Jesus brought us together. I was terribly aware of that last night. During these months of seeming absence (I knew he was closer than ever, but did not feel anything of him), I knew Jesus only in you, in the love of a brother and in the moments of reception of the Eucharist.

Friendship and Second Innocence

This reception of the Eucharist became terribly important to me for this reason, and I felt inconsolable when it did not come – when He did not come in this form, because He was not really in any other form. You remember the nightmares, the tortures of feeling abandoned, deserted by Him and sometimes by you that sometimes drove me to the point of suicide – and even to attempt that by omitting the medication. Last night I was perfectly calm and rational – this wasn't like a light, but it was a transformation of the darkness of the emptiness into a kind of fullness, a kind of strength, a return of presence that has sustained me all these years. I believe it began a year ago when we said that Mass together on the day of my departure, in your house. When it was over you moved to go toward the kitchen, taking me in the chair. I said, "No, wait a moment, something is happening inside of me." That day on the way to the airport you took off your glove and held my hand and said you felt at peace after I had told you that you were inhabiting those private places that only God had inhabited before.

Ours is a remarkable friendship in the sense that only you of all human beings have known me unveiled as Jesus knew me before. That was the reason for the great sense of privacy and secrecy – my previous inability to say one word about it. Who can ever speak of such things without realizing that no words are adequate to express them?

I told you that day of the Mass in your home that I love you as Jesus loved us. That was clear and real then. I have clung to that – loving and caring for you in your humanity, in your sore back, in your damaged feet. As the presence of Jesus grew less and less fresh in me during that dark night of the soul, as I had to come face to face with death and only you to share it, I became more and more desperate and frightened. Had my whole life been a delusion? Had all my theology been a lie that crumbled as the crunch came? I know from much reading of works by the saints that the only way to get through the purification was to remain faithful, even if it seemed the void. I tried with your companionship and guidance and help to do that. All of this leads up to saying that the thing that became clarified was somehow this: during this period of estrangement I loved you because the only Jesus I could find was the one indwelling in you. Last night, I realized that the "return" changed things subtly in that before I loved because of the Jesus within you, whereas now I could love you in Jesus Himself – surely a better love, one that can be more generous. I now love you because of the return of the presence within me and surrounding me. I love you in happiness and sanity rather than as my sole hope.

My gratitude is for you, that you have shared all of this with me in this agonizing year, and it is to God for the return of the sense of Jesus' presence in me and around me, permeating the atmosphere. Also to God, too, for sending me a real physical and spiritual brother to make the unbearable less unbearable.

John

November 2, 1977 – Feast of All Souls (John's journal)

I awakened as I went to sleep, aware of All Souls, which is every day for me, since I pray for souls I love and for those of people I love each day. Since few of my friends have been my contemporaries, the list grows longer as I grow older; my dad; my grandparents; Jacques, Vera and Raissa; Casadesus, Dominique Pire; Thomas Merton; John Murphy, CSB; Gerald Vann; Jean Hussar; Louis Liege; all my Jewish friends who perished in the Holocaust; Mary McKillop (and Tom because he was her husband and Tom's father); the Noonans' deceased relatives; Peter Geismar; the Sussmans' parents; John Turner's parents; Clyde Kennard; Pierre (and undoubtedly Henriette) Reverdy; Clyde Holland; George Levitan; the Markoe brothers; and those whom I knew less well but who were great heroes to me and formative influences on me – Roland Hayes; Martin Luther King; Bach and Mozart; Haydn, Schubert and Beethoven (more intimate than many of my friends).

John

✶✶

November 6, 1977

Hang in there, Tommy baby. Don't go to a psychotherapist who thinks that taking the Sermon on the Mount seriously constitutes a neurosis. The Minnesota tests were never designed for people with a passionate religious vocation. They were designed on the basis of "the average" rather than the truly normal.

John

November 8, 1977

Dear Tom,

There is the deeper starvation of this already mutilated physically affective life – and I just have to accept that as part of the picture. I think all helpless people must feel this; as do people like you – a tangible pain-filled longing to be loved, not sexually but physically – why this yearning, which is so deep it is an agony?

There is no more John left in me – there is only this struggling little Johnny, who is seen as finished in most people's eyes and who keeps yearning and hoping that there is a little something left of value in him, something he can still do. I accept and say yes to all of this, without resentment or bitterness, but with a terrible interior sadness. I offer that, which is worse than anything physical, for the intentions you already know, without any longer having the slightest assurance that the offering is worth a damn. It is a kind of fidelity and hope that I suppose will be the last remnants left in me by the time I leave this life.

May I be forgiven if my loving and caring are too much. They have never and do not now demand anything in return.

John

November 11, 1977

I know you are terribly busy, St. Tommy, and you have to have some time to rest and relax. I feel so happy about our friendship. I don't want it to be a burden to you. Write, tape or call just when you can and feel like it. We will be surrounding each other in prayer and in union of hearts.

John

November 12, 1977

Dear Tom,

God, what a need still burns in me to be helpful. As I see my family more and more starting already to build their new lives, I cannot help, for the love of them, to be grateful, though I felt abandoned for a time, and felt that despite this lived reality they were accepting something that somehow I did not want them to accept. All of that in a good way, but now I am almost without sorrow in this and at heart I am thankful. I only ask that you keep telling me to "hang in there, baby."

John

Friendship and Second Innocence

November 23, 1977

Dear Tom,

Talked with you on the phone last night and prayed and reflected about it for a long time afterward – your nervousness, your fatigue, your difficulty speaking and finally this thing adds up and becomes pretty clear. Everything ties in now, Tommy. I believe these tensions become damaging to you under one condition. The condition where you are suddenly rendered unfree, out of control of the situation, feeling pushed, coerced! Like me, you have a great and fierce thirst for freedom – interior freedom – and simply cannot bear to be placed in these straitjacket situations. I do not believe overwork does this, or even the most demanding challenges, so long as you can breathe and function freely. This ties in also with your slight claustrophobia.

You can face any problem without damage so long as it does not threaten that internal freedom that keeps you at peace with the challenge and with yourself there where it counts. I had once feared that you were just overworked and rested too little. I believe now that only damages you nervously and produces this dissonant kind of fatigue and misery in you when events and forces conspire to risk you with entrapment, where you are torn between your deep need to function freely and unfettered and when obligations of friendship, charity, etc., come into conflict with your principles and beliefs.

For people like us, sin is always a dissonant situation we are sometimes driven to it, but we suffer like hell afterward and feel unwhole until we get to confession.

The one thing that remains intact and grows, if we can handle the balance between dissonant and consonant situations, is the ability to become more and more free, more and more happy, more and more fulfilled and loving.

John

December 6, 1977

Dear Tom,

I am afraid it is a refuge of the mediocre that makes mediocre creativity and mediocre self the God, and some enslaving superficial quest for "freedom" on one's own terms the supreme virtue. What a tragedy this kind of reasoning proliferates.

All for the moment, blessed. Thank you for everything, especially for sharing with me and for carrying me in these days where sometimes that alone keeps me from simply giving up and doing something desperate. You cannot imagine how often, in those depths, just the sound of your voice, a word or phrase dropped here or there, memories of the past events of our friendship, and above all knowing that you are all right and thriving and functioning well, put the ground back under my feet, help me to find the courage to struggle back from the darkness of the confusion caused by pain and weakness.

John

December 6, 1977 (John's journal)

Although I paid no serious attention to the hate letter I received yesterday, I had the old nightmare again this morning. The "civilized" white mob converging on me mercilessly, to lynch me on the downtown lamppost in Mansfield as a protest against my work, which they say encourages "Negro savagery." My God, can any savagery equal the desires expressed in that hate letter? It is unspeakable. Others will tell me, "Don't pay attention to such sickies."

Well, I don't, but apparently my nightmares do and not without cause. I have viewed too many mutilated bodies that were the victims of their "savagery," along with all the sadism that accompanies it. Also, of course, the sickness of suggesting that any bad act by blacks is "Negro savagery," whereas the cruel, merciless, sadistic acts by whites are protection of "white civilization."

December 21, 1977 (John's journal)

I am not, God knows, opposed to community, but opposed to that concept of community that too often makes us unfree to fulfill the aspirations of individual vocations – in other words, community where one is obliged to listen to the will of the agglomerate rather than the will of God.

Reverdy said, "It is not mediocrity without vice that will give us a high degree of virtue." I think this kind of thing accounts for much of the acedia among the People of God, especially priests and religious; they need and thirst for something more than "mediocrity without vice," which too often is presented as the highest of goals and mistaken for virtue. Most of the "aware" ones are deeply distressed, often depressed, by this low norm. They feel unsupported in their ideals by their confreres and colleagues until finally the ideal sinks to that level of conformity and acceptance that is common. This is always accompanied by a sense of defeat, a sense of compromise in being far less real and therefore far less individual, far less themselves.

December 30, 977

Dear John,

Msgr. Lacey is coming up this morning, bringing the mail – hopefully some of yours and to hear my confession. We'll also talk about the letter to the Senate that I mentioned in yesterday's letter.

I was so happy that the tape I sent was helpful to you. It always seems that there are special moments when speaking in the first person, though hopefully not presumption, flows out in spite of the clogged filter, to help and heal. At those times, Jesus simply speaks using my imagination and directing what is said specifically to the person. I feel deeply appreciative that something said was of internal value to you, especially when your heart was doing a hop, skip and a jump. I was never very good at that field event – I always got mixed up.

Mass is now and I'll offer it up especially for you – this is not a special saint's day so perhaps Jesus can take you and me as No. 2s to fill up the vacuum before Mother Teresa, Pope John, Dorothy Day or Baroness Catherine de Hueck Doherty fills it up.

Have a peaceful and healing new year.

Sincerely in Jesus,

Tom

1978

January 1, 1978

Interview with John Howard Griffin

Hope for the Future? "My God, If We Only Had a Few Saints"
Catholic New Times, p. 2

Christmas night, John Howard Griffin and Fr. Tom McKillop from Toronto sat in Griffin's home and talked about what lies ahead in 1978. John Howard Griffin lives with his wife and three of their four children in Fort Worth, Texas.

He is ailing and Fr. McKillop came from Toronto to spend the Christmas holidays with him.

The following is an interview done especially for *Catholic New Times* in which John Howard Griffin reflects on the future:

Fr. McKillop: Thinking of Jacques Maritain, Fr. Gerald Vann, Fr. Dominique Pire and of Fr. Thomas Merton, who were important influences in your life, what would they say today of the future?

John Howard Griffin: I think if they had to boil it down to one statement, they might agree that future hopes are in direct ratio to mankind's ability to overcome our greatest temptation – which is the temptation to try to do good without God. We have a thirst to be good in and of ourselves. I don't really know why, but I do know that it never works. This is proved by the fact that so many of our good efforts die on the vine. I think in this connection of the "do-gooders" who join every cause and try their hand at everything but who constantly play out, grow tired, give up and move on to something else. People like Maritain, Vann, Pire and Merton perceived and understood the hopelessness of pursuing the temptation to "do good without God," the absolute necessity of constantly seeking guidance from the Holy Spirit and remaining faithful to that guidance. All would admit that they were lost on their own without it. What will keep us persevering in the future will be fidelity to and dependence on that same guidance of the Holy Spirit.

Fr. McKillop: Where would these men and yourself see hope in the future?

Griffin: My God, if we only had a few saints! Humans thirst for hope through such examples. We would find hope in the few people who have vision and comprehension. What would help others to persevere would be these examples. Archbishop Helder Camara of Recife, Brazil, has called them the Abrahamic minorities. To me, these are the people who first of all have a vision of the sufferings of humanity and see them at the level of the prophets. Therefore they see the need of healing the wounds of others for the love of others and of God. They are the ones who try to help people deal with their sense of existential vacuum, and with barriers to communications across racial, cultural and religious differences. Hope for the future depends on the expansion of the Abrahamic minority.

Fr. McKillop: What directions can we go?

Griffin: We can go one of two ways. We can fail to be willing to live through disillusionment in ourselves without God and end up in utter despair. Or we can pass through our disillusionment and come to the conviction that we need to have a profound and real relationship with God. Those who try the second way are the ones who never extinguish and finally make a lifetime commitment and cling safely to it. They work for the good of the work or need rather than simply for the good of themselves.

Fr. McKillop: What is the turning point?

Griffin: The turning point is that humiliating moment when we come to realize that no matter how hard we try to do good by ourselves, we bungle and fail; that can also be the moment of grace. Maritain said that that's the moment when we realize that some of us may be called to be martyrs for the love of our neighbours, that we consider no sacrifice too great. That is the moment, too, when the beatitudes make supreme sense because we are called to live them, to risk being misunderstood, spat upon. We shift from admiring the beatitudes to living them. We give ourselves away, so to speak, by making ourselves dependent on and pliable to the will of God. That is the ultimate freedom.

Fr. McKillop: What stops us?

Griffin: Love of self, which is good and necessary, provided we don't just stop there ... when we do some good act for some conscious or unconscious good for ourselves all in appearing to do it for the good of others. This spoils it.

Fr. McKillop: What frees us?

Griffin: Authentic love which truly desires the good of another over the good of oneself.

Fr. McKillop: If you were selecting one area of concentration for 1978, what would it be?

Griffin: It would be salvaging the young and therefore ourselves. We can look at younger people in one of three ways. First, we can say that they are no damn good – let them wallow in it. Second, we can do damage by not accepting them at their level but always wanting them to be at our level. Third, we don't have to wait for them to be adults to be our brothers and sisters. It is this third way which is the way ... to talk, share, work and pray with them rather than at them. We become co-helpers in facing and overcoming the problems in the one spirit. In a word, as Vann himself said, and Merton also in different language, "In the realm of the Spirit, what we do is less important than what we allow to be done to us."

January 6, 1978 (John's journal)

When I was here alone with Tom, he kept pressing hard on the left ventricle of my heart with one hand and guided my breathing with his hand on my abdomen, pressing and releasing, reminding me to breathe in rhythm to the pressure and release. From a great distance I would hear his calm voice, saying, "Squeeze my arm, John" and that would bring me back enough to try to obey, to concentrate on doing something. When I could no longer see anything but a fuzzy image of his face, he lowered his head close so I could see his eyes, remind me to pray, anything to keep me attached to the real and bring me back from the distance. The sadness was replaced with a profound sense of gratitude as he seemed to bring me back by the sheer force of his efforts, his inventiveness.

I think of this relationship with much fascination. Clinically, the chances are that I will never see him again, and yet I feel no sense of farewell. When you have gone through the intimate reality of death together – how many times now? – a unique kind of bonding takes place that time and distance and death cannot really affect; the friendship somehow becomes both sacramental and totally transparent, so that there is as much ease together as there is usually only when one is alone. Here my helplessness is in the hands of a beloved friend. The thing I detest about the prospect of going to the hospital is that my helplessness is in the hands of strangers – always a profound humiliation and embarrassment. At least at home my helplessness is in the hands of family and friends, but here the tendency is always to protect them as much as possible from the rawness of all this – something I cannot manage very well at times. It does little good to try to reassure them when they find you nearly unconscious or come in and see you in pain that no one could hide.

Friendship and Second Innocence

January 16, 1978 (John's journal)

Deep longing for someone to laugh with; the feelings in me were too dead, too heavy.

January 18, 1978

Dear Tom,

I pray for you and your intentions with my words and with my weakness. I pray that our deep friendship has given you something of the reality of the love of Jesus, as it has me ... something of the tenderness and sharing of the incarnation, something of true love that is both Jesus-centred and human-centred, something of that rare, authentic twinship and brotherhood that will carry us through our weaknesses and help both of us to experience Jesus as our Beloved Brother through all our good and bad moments in life, always with us. I look up to see a heavy snow falling outside the windows.

John

✱ ✱

January 24, 1978

Dear Tom,

In another week, you will have your birthday, and this letter will probably get there about that time. It is a momentous one, the 50th, the beginning of real maturity, I think, and for you a time of great richness and growth and youth.

John

**

January 31, 1978 (John's journal)

On this birthday, I pray, "God hold him, pet him, love him, and make him know and feel it."

**

February 15, 1978

Dear Old Tommy,

I enclose this morning's journal notes, which tell of the extraordinary coincidence in the middle of the night when I was in terrible pain and turned on the TV for something to distract me. There was Dr. Kübler Ross – it was almost like a visit from you. I hope these notes are helpful to you in bringing you "inside," so to speak ... anyway, they are part of the sharing of brothers. Also, you might like to know how you are perceived. Even if I did not see you as part of me, even if our profound affection did not exist, I would still see you the same for your understanding and help, just as I feel as though Dr. Kübler-Ross, Dr. Ford, etc., are doing a very great work, a blessed work, so desperately needed if we are to make dying not a gratuitous torture.

The radiation (another today and then one more) is helping. No vomiting this morning, no bleeding, fulsome number 2, first normal one this week; and so far no loss of body hair which they said sometimes (not always) occurs.

But trouble in the weakness – strange – the part that gets more than its share of oxygenated blood – resisted last night and today but it is constantly popping up (literally & figuratively) in dreams, thoughts, sudden images. More and more I feel that to fall into this, no matter how great the pressure, somehow deprives someone of some grace, though I am reconciled enough to it when it is happening and I keep trying, as you say, to "move on" afterward and not fall into self-centred mourning, although that aftermath feeling is perhaps the deepest unhappiness I know right now. When you are so physically "unwhole" the desire to be otherwise whole is perhaps accentuated.

I hope you feel a sense of my presence there as I sense your presence here. It comes especially in bad moments when I see you sitting beside me on the bed, holding me, blessing the areas of pain, talking, looking at me, sharing and lessening the morbid aspects. I carry the hanky constantly in my left-side pajama pocket exactly as I carry the nitro with me there. It seems to me that when I get lost in the images and cannot keep little Johnny tucked in, all the good presences vanish – which is perhaps why the pleasure is a bitter one. I would rather keep the sense of presence than do anything to lose it, even temporarily, even momentarily.

Looking at some of the pictures of Sharon yesterday, I was reminded to mention something to you and probably the Sharon team. In some of these pictures I am parked in my wheelchair beside that lovely lady who was in her wheelchair, and I was left up there beside her the night of the candlelighting ceremony. I am too weak to explain correctly, but you will understand when I suggest that this is not really a good idea. My experience indicates that handicapped people are always put together, as though the handicap somehow united them. People are drawn to one another as people, and prefer to gravitate toward those they like. It used to infuriate me to see the way they always put the blind together – and it infuriates many handicapped people ... it's a kind of segregation. I have never felt united to anyone because of a similarity of handicaps, and I have always sensed a kind of degradation to be dumped together with another handicapped person just because you are limited in a similar way. I have known as many blind sonsofbitches as sighted ones, as many handicapped ones as whole ones. That lady and I both felt a kind of uneasiness in being placed so arbitrarily together by well-meaning people. I was very distraught by this that night when finally I tried to wheel myself back to the cabin and Charlie caught up with me and pushed the wheelchair. It was pitiful because she tried to "console" me and held my hand and I suppose I did the same with her, and I know both of us felt the utter falsity of trying to "do our duty." Since you, old brother, work so extensively with the handicapped, I would think about this and perhaps share it with those with whom you work.

For the physically limited, it is degrading, because many of us do not consider ourselves necessarily unwhole otherwise. I used to be criticized because I refused to attend more than one dinner for "the blind." I felt that kind of thing was the utter shredding of any dignity whatsoever and always condemned it in my writings for the American Foundation for the Blind. Let your handicapped gravitate toward those with whom they feel the most comfortable, whether that be a fellow handicapped person or (more likely) one who has what we do not have. It's nothing against either myself or that lady to say that every time we were "put together" and then left there by those who handled our chairs we felt all kinds of tensions and unspoken disappointment ... not to be together, but to be put together precisely because others thought we should be together and placed us continually in that clumsy situation.

You know I tell you that only to be of help, not to criticize at all. It is rather, I should imagine, like being segregated with fellow human beings because they happen to be priests at some function, even though you would just as soon be with lay people and even though your priesthood does not guarantee that you are drawn to each other (maybe on the contrary).

No one likes to be a "condition"; we want to be "*persona*." I found, on the other hand, during my blindness, that if people (sighted people, I mean) did not manipulate us, we made many friends among the fellow blind, but this was not because of the blindness but because of our qualities as human individuals.

All for the moment, old buddy.

God love you and keep you.

Love,

Johnny

February 15, 1978 (John's journal)

I once wrote last year that my experience with total helplessness and pain – the extreme vulnerability of being completely stripped and half-maddened – made me realize that the fine points of theological and philosophical speculation that have fascinated me all of my life were all reduced to two words: love and innocence. I did not mean innocence in the small sense of sexual virtue but in the large sense of purity of heart.

February 21, 1978 (John's journal)

I finally went to sleep saying prayers of penance, hearing you say, "We have to move on."

February 24, 1978

Dear Tom,

I feel flashes of loss in the human separation, which has to be, of course, but a loss in not being able to take care of you, to fix your back, to fix your feet, to fix your scalp and the back of your neck, etc. An almost incessant feeling of gratitude that you are a priest, a committed brother; how your priesthood deepens the love we hold for one another, blesses in a very real sense. I don't think I could ever have been this close with anyone else, nor have I ever for a moment forgotten your priesthood and particularly the loneliness of an essential aspect of priesthood – a loneliness I have hoped to partially mitigate.

John

✶ ✶

February 28, 1978

Dear Old Tommy,

A quick note to tell you that I hope you are taking good care of that 'flu. It is dangerous to start to work when you are just slightly better and then have a relapse.

Fr. Stan called last night to say Tony Walsh had accepted the CCS Gold Medal Award; and also to say that *Our Sunday Visitor* picked up our interview in *Catholic New Times*. What did we do wrong, Tom? Anyway, they did a resumé of it with most of my quotes, apparently, and plugged *New Times*, but the beasts did not even mention your name, and the one really good part about the whole thing was that we worked *together* on it. They said *New Times* visited me at Christmas. Are you *New Times*? They issued the thing as a News Bulletin, as I understand it. I am really pissed off with this kind of journalistic sloppiness.

I am enclosing an interesting clipping from Dr. Ford about US charismatics (which she specifies does not apply to Canadian charismatics ... yet). She is a great lady, like Kübler-Ross. She had a hell of a time getting into Canada when she went to lecture for Fr. Stan at Windsor.

Fr. Stan also sent the *Man Alive* show with Hans Küng, which I have been too sick to hear until perhaps today. If you missed it, and it is decently recorded, I'll send it along, although I have the impression it was not too interesting.

Friendship and Second Innocence

Thank you, blessed, for carrying me through this impossible period. Every time I have woken up in the last 24 hours, I have managed to think instantly of praying before the more troublesome thoughts could become destructive, but in the extreme pain, I have great difficulty doing that, and can sometimes only say "Yes."

Pray for the repose of my old friend, the very great artist Abraham Rattner, who died at age 83 on Saturday. We have been friends since the late '30s and crossed to America from France on the same boat in 1940. He was the one who helped me like a father through the Eartha Kitt humiliation. (Along with his wonderful wife who died about ten years ago.) Although Jewish, he was unfailingly supportive of me in my religious longings and later in my work. A great artist and a saintly man.

Stay close in concentration this next week, from Wednesday, when you fly to Thunder Bay – and I will offer all of this for whatever intentions you have and for your well-being.

Love,

Walrus

March 4, 1978

Dear John:

    Penn Jones
    Varsity News
    Strong comments Maybe
    overstated. Feeling
    angst Talked to Jim
    Nothing's happened

Bishop hasn't called.
On way to
New Times
Report this Afternoon
– wonder! Tape
completed Sent to
you. Your beautiful
tape Almost finished
Tonight will Do it.
A trail of discouragement
Runs through my cranium The
effect of non response. This
time has me Though
intellectually I see the
irrationality of it all.
Praying for closeness
In Jesus
And Friends.
The time
Presses forward
Responsibilities ahead
Walked to the Cathedral
Reflecting the talks For
Warkworth On Search,
Sharing and Faith.
Your resistance
And fortitude
A quiet witness
Of strength. The
Heart Paining
you Yet Jesus
Seemingly healing you.

> My body sensitized
> Probably vulnerable To
> the heartaches Of you,
> Jim Maybe mostly
> Myself. Hope Self-pity
> Not sinking
> Into me.
> Yet the main
> Presses outward
> Needing peace
> Ease –
> Not much
> Humour
> Just my
> Self this day.

Love

Tom

March 7, 1978 (John's journal)

Dr. Kyger said tonight I have three fatal diseases: thickening of the arteries, degenerating heart disease, and the unspeakable one, all aggravated by the diabetes.

March 7, 1978 (John's notes)

I think of things about young men who have inordinate spiritual ambitions (what other words are there?). So many come to see me, having heard the message and "deciding to become saints temporarily" (and comfortably and on their own terms). Another statement from Verba Seniorum comes to mind: Certain old men (Desert Fathers) said, "If thou see-est a young man ascending by his own will up to heaven, catch him by the foot and throw him down upon the earth" (V.S.V. of X. p. 107) – which means put him back in touch with some reality, with what is real.

St. Bernard remarked in this connection, "In the light of God, one learns what one does not know; one does not unlearn what one knows." When one unlearns what one knows in error, that is innocence; when one simply obliterates what one knows, that is ignorance and delusion, even when attempted (and it is often done) in some misguided sense of virtue.

Later: past midnight. I do not try to see the clock.

Hunger: I try to think what I can have that will assuage it. I have a memory of my dad, and realize how like him I am becoming. Things he ate that seemed so poor to me. Now I feel the urge to eat similar things. I soften some crackers in stewed tomatoes (cold), and slowly consume that with a glass of milk. It is good. Perhaps if I can get over the hunger, I will sleep after all.

March 8, 1978 (John's notes)

Now it must be March 8, though it is still only an hour or so after midnight. Feast of one of my patrons, St. John of God. "The Son gives life to anyone he chooses," says the Gospel. Sometimes I wonder how it is that I continue to live, that in fact I have lived through many deaths, or death sentences. I think it is the countless prayers of friends, known and unknown to me.

How strange a feast night. I had to wait for the crackers to soften more before I could go on with my little feast. I sit here in some hourless night before dawn by several hours. The whole family sleeps, all of my beloved friends hopefully sleep in their beds around the country and in Canada. I alone seem to be awake in this lamplight, reading the Mass texts for this day, in a deep, deep silence. Then I eat my crackers and tomatoes and hope for sleep. No troubles this night, nothing disturbing in my thoughts or desires ... a kind of contentment. I pray it is the same for those I love. Cold. I pull the covers up over my shoulders and am shaken with occasional rigours. In my mind, a hand calms them, a hand on my chest, near my heart.

It occurs to me that the part of me that had a true hermit vocation is perhaps realized in this illness that isolates me from nearly all living activity. If so, then it is a gift from God, perhaps a profound favour from Him that I have not understood. I think of Merton's "I seek to become a no-one in order to be united in love to everyone." Tonight, in this solitude and silence, I feel a close kinship to those feelings I have had in times of more healthy and active solitude. The illness that walls me in and makes me more and more helpless and isolated is perhaps what God provides as my cell. It is a vocation poorly understood, much feared, and little esteemed these days. I am like the fish of Abbot Anthony (in Verba Seniorum) who left the sea to live in the world: all these years I have lived in the world of social action, because of obedience to the will of God and the love I have in such measure within me. Now that life is finished, "As a fish must return to the sea, so must we to our cell: lest it befall that by tarrying without, we forget the watch within" (V.S. Book II, p. 63). In this sense, it occurs to me that perhaps it is through this illness that God returns me to my cell ... at least that makes some sense.

My hands are tired from typing, but the perceptions and memories continue to come. Some people, certainly Christ, are destined to love others more wholly and completely than others are capable of loving them in return.

✻ ✻

March 12, 1978 (John's notes)

Though I relish what is robust and real and tender in love, its proper earthiness when shared by two people who are deep friends and who trust one another with the precious gift of simply being themselves, I despise the cheapness that tarnishes so much of what today passes for love, so often self-seeking, self-serving. Such love can never have the heroic quality of caring always for the good of the beloved rather than for the good of self. This always, ultimately, leads to treachery against the loved one.

Why do I continue to be put off by people who write and speak so glibly about Jesus, as though they were saying and writing what they thought should be said and written? Such homages often remind me of the Chamber of Commerce's honouring of prominent men, who are always paragons of all the virtues, regardless of their reality. It remains nearly impossible for me to write or say the name, even though for many years the most natural and comfortable of prayers for me has been the Jesus Prayer: Blessed Lord Jesus, Son of God, have mercy on me, a poor sinner. In the last couple of years I have changed that last to "have mercy on us poor sinners," because the emphasis on me does not sit right.

All report that communication continues. I have experienced this palpably. I recall when Piedy's father died. Bess called down to our house and asked if I knew how to give artificial resuscitation. I flew out of our house and ran up the pathway, even though both feet were bandaged from recent surgery. I seemed to fly toward him, feeling no pain in my still-stitched feet, which broke open and bled all over the place. I felt a terrible loss and panic and began to weep while running and I clearly heard his voice saying, "You can do better than that, son." It immediately set me right and I went about the task of trying to resuscitate him with great calm and love and efficiency, but of course it was too late.

Also, I have long ago realized that I have been near death many times, and was always astonished to come out of comas still alive, or out of operations still alive. I suppose the ideal of trying to create some hint of heaven on earth was the driving force of all my work since that first slow come-back from that first bombing.

March 16, 1978 (John's notes)

I think that my great final friendship with Tom, which evolved naturally and was not deliberate, was at base a movement towards a relationship that could be total and yet be a sharing foretaste of heaven in all the reality of life, an attempt to share that core of loneliness that is in all of us when we face the ultimates and few can be with us totally in that final part, no matter how much they have loved us in our living. Part of the great difficulty of undergoing great pain is not just the pain, but the struggles to protect others from sights they cannot take. What they call withdrawal is really, in my experience, the fear of others' withdrawal, which is unbearable, and so we do the withdrawing. Most of the time I feel utterly alone except in union of prayers, sharing and affection with those who can come into this agony with me; most of those who have been nearest to me in life cannot come all this way. Only one has been able to come all this way with me. The others do their duty, watch and wait, lovingly but also with a certain profound distaste, shock, even dread. They accept grimly what happens to me and face it as best they can, with a great and terrible ache. I suppose that is the best we can do with such a situation. Tom comes with me all the way, and even gives me the privilege of helping him as I can; and allows me the blessing of feeling no embarrassment or humiliation with some of these grosser aspects of physical degeneration and death.

March 19, 1978 – Palm Sunday (John's journal)

No strength, no nothing. I make these notes for whatever reason, just as I go on with some of the other relics of living when I feel no more living in me.

Week of days and night fading into one another in a daze: not the daze of sedation, for everything is felt with uncushioned acuity, but daze of being inside, doubled up in pain, in a kind of harrowing loneliness that nothing seems to reach.

The big obligations I can no longer fulfill, so the tiniest ones become like big ones: obligation to be patient, to answer questions, to eat occasionally, to run a wet cloth over my face and brush my teeth; sometimes to talk on the phone.

Visit yesterday from Deba Patnaik, surely one of the world's choicest people. I dreaded it, tried to put it off; but when he came I was unfailingly moved during every moment of his stay.

How many times this week did I lie in the quiet of my bed and hear through the closed door outbursts of laughter from the living room, hearing people talk in the distance, make plans and projects and feel myself utterly disconnected from such ways of being and thinking and planning.

Talk less and less. Piedy does nearly all the talking on the phone now. I talk only to certain old friends, like Fr. Tom, Fr. Stan, the Noonans – people like that.

One night this week, in desperation, unable to breathe, I got up and sat in the living room while everyone slept. Warm, clear night. I moved to the door and then stepped outside on the porch – warmth, darkness, freshness of the air. I looked up at the stars and could not bear the sight. I shrivelled up inside, quickly closed the door against the sight and returned into the shelter away from the vastness.

Painful realization, which I accept because that is how it is: I become a tinier and tinier part of my friends' and family's works. Life's demands, pleasures, preoccupations and companions occupy more and more of their reality and I less and less. Many have long since made the adjustment to live without me; for many I am dead, but not yet buried. It is proper that it be so, even though it is sometimes heartbreakingly painful to be on the diminishing end. You get the feeling that you receive whatever time is left over, or can be crowded into their lives. Far worse, you feel a kind of sickish gratitude even for those scraps. I know that people out there, a handful, carry me in their hearts through the days and nights; that many stay fixed on other things because they feel so saddened or else so uncomfortable or often uneasy around the dying.

And the absurdities: At this moment Fr. George called. Wanted to know if I were having a good day. I told him no. He said he would come by to see me. He had just found a recipe for zucchini meat loaf (dear God) from *The Zucchini Cookbook*.

Palm Sunday today: hot, dark, windy, a sense of apprehension and even dread for the feelings always elicited in me by Holy Week. Those are feelings, at least. Last year Fr. Tom came to help me through Holy Week and see me into Easter. This year I go with it alone, more alone than I have ever been in my life. That, too, is part of it.

I do not mean to sound as though I were complaining, but much of what warmed the heart out of a kind of spontaneous love a year ago now chills the heart because the same things are done out of a sense of duty, charity. The difference is appalling. I am sure that all terminal people feel this (even when it may not be true). It is part of the desolation of no longer being connected with life.

Yet there are moments when I am connected. I continue to take delight in reading Joe Noonan's letters and the Sussmans' letters ... and a few others. My big sense of responsibility comes now in taking care of the plants inside. Feeling like death itself this morning, I watered and pruned. My sight is seriously diminished and usually blurred, but for one brief moment this morning, the freshness of a few drops of water that got on the geranium leaves brought everything into focus: a remarkably beautiful, life-giving clarity that lasted only a moment, but it shocked me that I could still feel such things, and for a few seconds I felt whole.

The danger of living up to images others create of us, of drifting into that falsity; those who have an authentic piety and simple, direct belief; who become known for it and who try to live up to that and become merely pietistic and hollow, saying the things they do not feel, that are untrue to them.

What sappiness: people who act macho; people who say "golden things" because their faith has turned back on them and is no longer a spotlight to guide them, but only a stage-spot to illuminate them to the audience of the world; the obligations we sincerely place upon the dying, who try to do so decently. At least by talking to them they can find meaning in their death as a means of edifying the living.

Fr. G. came, brought me some homemade bread. It turned into a very good visit, in fact. I was slugging coffee, trying to get some strength. He offered to fix me more. I thanked him, told him I was coffeed out.

"Does it give you a lift?" he asked.

"I guess so – at least I have the illusion it does," I said.

From old habit, he jumped at the chance. "You know they say that cayenne pepper is almost the best heart stimulus there is ..."

I began to draw in, barricade myself from another health-food-herb assault. "In *Search for Eden* the author contends that cayenne pepper is a wonderful heart-strengthener," he went on.

"Father," I said, more amused than irritated, "haven't you come to realize yet that I no longer have any interest in finding some Eden?"

He reacted very well, saying, "Oh, I know ... these things sound silly, don't they. You are surrounded by all these claims made by people who have no proof whatsoever. This search for Eden is kind of pathetic in your eyes and in your condition, I know."

I thought of the one Eden I do know – Sharon; for a moment I felt a great longing to go there. But no, I am no longer able to take care of myself and I cannot ask others to go on taking care of me. Tom, the only one who could, is more and more absorbed with the living. And that is right (though it sometimes leaves a forlorn feeling), and I would not have it any other way.

Perhaps the most desolating thing that occurs in those who die slowly is the attrition of affections in those who love them. Slowly, tangibly, you feel yourself being shifted from the affectionate, loving centres of people's hearts to places on their duty rosters. This is the central agony of dying slowly. No one wants to be on anyone's duty roster. No one who has experienced the lifegiving blessings of love can bear to have it turn into charity, duty. Contacts

Mother Teresa speaks at a Youth Corps event. Jean Vanier is at the far left of the photograph.

that were beautiful in the context of love become unbearable in the context of duty.

I think the above explains the true genius of Mother Teresa in her work. I cannot help but wonder why the great studies on death and dying exclude (as far as I know) all of this: they still make judgments from the viewpoint of the living rather than from that of the dying. They talk of withdrawal; the great agony of the dying is the other's withdrawal from us, it seems to me.

Another point that comes clearer and clearer: the religious dimension. I am not at all sure it really diminishes, even though it appears to. Rather, a great reconciliation between pietism and a deeper, straighter truth seems to emerge that reveals all those scabs of unreality under which so many religiously centred hide for security. Becker has many truths here. When those security scabs are finally melted in the fires of dying, religious dimensions change appearances, become perhaps whole for the first time. To suggest that this is sweet is insane. It is terrible to go through: it leaves us naked of all consolation. For those in life who think we fade away blissfully in Jesus' arms to the music of angelic choirs, perhaps that delusion can remain in a quick death without the interminable crucifixion. But when the dying is long, it fades to the other; and this seems to bring about disappointment on the part of the living.

I expect that only the saints could sustain ardent love under the circumstances. We can all sustain it when death is not prolonged, rallying everything to pour love into the dying. All of that fades when death is prolonged. The living go on using the word "love," when what they communicate is only duty. To the dying, from whom all props and supports gradually erode, the quality of and the expressions for and the signs of love become supremely important.

Those who gradually draw away sometimes feel that we always have the warmth of Jesus' presence, but with each withdrawal of a beloved person, we feel the simultaneous withdrawal of Jesus' presence. That is the harsh, nasty truth; and I think that is why the seeming withdrawal of beloved persons becomes a double disaster for us. We experience Jesus' love through the very presence and reality of human love. To think that we can feel loved by Jesus and unloved by beloved friends is so utterly false. So when we are shifted from hearts to daily rosters, when loved ones get "too busy," then the diminution of presence is the double diminution of the presence, warmth, tenderness, reality, spontaneity of their human/divine/love. This is automatically the deprivation of any of these same qualities, in regard to the presence and love of Jesus.

It is a hot and silent Sunday afternoon. How clumsily and laboriously I have made these notes and now I wonder why. Only the living can read them and I doubt if the living can possibly "come inside" and understand them. The tendency is always to judge the dying by those hollow criteria that make sense only to the living. Where does "bravery" come in? Hell, "He's not being very brave!" Hell, don't you know he can't be?

This is why the value judgments of the living, the "search for Eden" bullshit of the living, often sound so hopeless to the dying. Sometimes you have the forlorn feeling that 99 per cent of life's dreams, aspirations, goals are unconscious flight from death, obfuscation of death ... rather than something authentic in themselves.

March 22, 1978

Dear Johnny,

> As I sit here
> And leave the
> Telephone down
> And Feel your
> Great Support
> And love

1978

I simply streak
A few lines Of
ink
Knowing that I
Haven't written
For a while
But the intensity
Has simply been
Overwhelming. My
arm is alright My
work socks Were
simply Too tight
And they probably
Caused the pain
Around the legs.
It's been an
Incredible time
For action And
tomorrow We're
having One day
with Jim and
Shelley Douglass
on Spirituality
and Resistance.
We're now Sexists
and I Told you And
may
Have an
Evaluation of
What happened
Tomorrow night.
I have 12 journals

Complete now
And it's flowing well.
I hope to carry on As
best as I can. A
journal a week Seems
to be the Pace or
better Than that at
The moment. It's been
A rich experience
Doing it.
The next two weeks
Seem to be Giving
the Sight of some
Break – I hope It
can work and Also
for you.
Sorry for shortness.

Peace and love,

Tommy

✶ ✶

March 25, 1978

Dear Johnny,

You seemed
Clear yet
Groggy last night
As we talked Of
Jane Fonda Your

tasks To be done
And your
Personal sickness,
I hope
That you're
Given the strength
To do
Those check points
For the journal.
Thank God The
future Always
demand a response.
Wouldn't it Be
great
To have You
here For the
Octoberfest
With the
Taize experience.
So many
Ask of you
And your condition
And seem
Deeply concerned. You
have so Many
concerned Contacts
and friends In
Toronto.
Keep the old bod
Together and get Ready
for the Contemplation in
Action In that country

> That you
> Reacted against
> So often in
> Your earlier journals

Peace and love,

Tommy

March 26, 1978

Dear John,

The flight plans are as follows:

> Leave Toronto: Monday, April 4th
> 8:05 a.m. Flight 796 – Air Canada
> 11:05 a.m. Arrive in Dallas

Tentatively

> Leave Dallas: Monday, April 11th
> 4:05 p.m. Flight 797 – Air Canada
> 7:45 p.m. Arrive in Toronto

Holy Week will be one of the most beautiful this year, and I'm deeply looking forward to being with you and your beautiful family. It comes at a right time for me because of the avalanche of commitments I've had. I should not complain because I know from personal experience of sickness how precious life is, how precious strength is, the opportunity of being able to communicate, to help, to love. Having said this, it'll be great to be and to love and be loved. I'll send this right away to get to you immediately.

Sincerely in Christ,

Tom

1978

April 21, 1978 (John's journal)

Trying to make notes; first time in a long time. Have slept almost 24 hours under heavy sedation for the pain. It is better than taking that damned dope.

Some days I cannot leave the bed; some days I spend a good deal of time out there seated, feeling the sun on me. I gradually get the cuttings potted – although frequently it takes me all day to pot two of them. I feel a marvellous gratitude that something grows and flowers from this. I am reading books on horticulture and agriculture from the library, the most interesting one dating from 1856; but very thorough and scientific.

June 16, 1978 (John's journal)

My 58th birthday. Astonishment to have reached it. On my 57th birthday, celebrated in Toronto, there seemed little chance.

Remembered by my friends ("when we think of each other we somehow see each other"). Call from Sr. Gwen last night, talked with Tom last night, remembrances from the Noonans, the Sussmans, Fr. Stan, Fr. Clayton and all my family. These things mean life.

August 2, 1978 (John's journal)

Long reflection at Communion, as I prayed for all my friends, each by name, and for those who are mortally ill, particularly Maxwell Geismar, Don Burton, and others whom I do not know personally: Sr. St. Raymond, the child who is dying of cancer about whom Dan Berrigan wrote, the people who are caring for him in ultimus and for all the patients at the St. Rose of Lima home for those dying of incurable cancer. Prayed especially for Tom at the University of Peace, as I do so often, that he be filled with all the graces necessary to fulfill his great vocation. Also that I be a support in this for the rest of my life and forever. I prayed in this context for all those heroic enough to sacrifice a lot of temporal values for the healing of the world's wounds, mostly self-inflicted.

August 6, 1978 – Feast of the Transfiguration (John's journal)

My son Greg's 21st birthday and my daughter Susie and Steve's second anniversary, so we had them all over for a joint celebration dinner. I had foot surgery yesterday, but managed to sit at the table and share the meal, which was excellent:

- Homemade cream of leek soup
- Fondu Bourguignon (made with tenderloin and served with a Béarnaise sauce
- Fresh broccoli, buttered; tiny carrots glazed and parsleyed
- Mixed fresh peaches and strawberries, in Kirsch with whipped cream
- The birthday and anniversary cakes.

Everyone was here, including Marco and Mother and later Linda Kay.

I miss writing to people, but cannot write to Tom because he is probably en route to Taizé or L'Arche and then back to Toronto on Monday the 14th.

It is true, however, that you can love a near stranger. Certainly, I met Mary McKillop at the very end of her life and I know we felt an instant communication that was mutual. It was immediately as if we had known each other forever. I think this can happen. It depends on the ratio of falsity that is involved in the communication with one another. I held her hand and kissed her on the cheek because I wanted to, not because to do so was ordained by some damned specialist. If I had done so for any other reason, the falsity would have been clear to her and it would have been painful for her.

September 21, 1978 (John's journal)

Two magnificent weeks in Toronto with Fr. Tom, where we managed, in spite of heart attack and the growing, finally exploding, tumour, we managed to accomplish together things I am too far gone even to think of accomplishing alone. How I wish I had the strength to note it all down. Two weeks of life – in spite of the reality of this physical condition.

1979

April 24, 1979 (John's journal)

My first attempt to write more than notes for eight weeks, since I entered the hospital. While in the hospital they severed my right leg just below the knee. I went in weighing 190 lbs and now weigh 158 lbs. I still sleep about 20 hours a day, and someone has to be in the house in case of need — I have fallen severely three times. I take physical therapy twice a week, and am learning some skills — like how to take a bath in a tub.

The only visitor I can have for a long time is Fr. Tom McKillop, who was here until the day I entered the hospital.

Now the left leg is healing nicely and the doctors are watching carefully to see that the right leg does not go the same way. It seems to be improving.

April 27, 1979 (John's journal)

Got a call from Tom and another from the Sussmans last evening, and for some reason I was filled with a sorrow to make you weep. Why? Because I felt I would not see any of them again. But today has been all right, after a good sleep.

May 1, 1979 (John's journal)

Even more strange are the phantom pains I have had today — severe pains in my right foot (the one that is gone). They are real: they feel exactly as they did before the foot was severed, but they occur seldom, thank God.

Even though I have a little more typing facility, my texts, no matter how careful, are full of errors. This is one reason I continue typing, even though I have nothing important to say.

May 13, 1979 – Mother's Day (John's journal)

We celebrated with an outdoor cookout (though we ate inside). Now, at 5:30 p.m., everyone is taking a nap.

Piedy cut my hair this morning and I was hoping for some help in taking a shower, but not this time.

May 16, 1979 (John's journal)

Piedy and I are sick as dogs – a form of flu or bad cold that spreads all over town.

May 27, 1979 (John's journal)

Tom is at Sharon, I expect, working on The Beatitudes talks. Last week he put some difficult questions directly to me, and I have been thinking of them ever since. What I wouldn't give to hear what he ends up saying at the conference – I may have been unrealistic in my answers. If so, he will catch them.

Chief Dan George with Fr. Terry Gallagher at a 1979 Youth Corps event

October 14, 1979 (John's journal)

The big day in Toronto, with Fr. Tom having Chief Dan George and Prof. Handa. He strongly invited me. I would have given anything to have gone, but this time it is obviously impossible. Slept very little last night.

October 23, 1979 – Feast of St. Juan Capistrano (John's journal)

It is past 3:00 p.m. and only now have I been able to leave the bed long enough to make these notes and rebandage my eyes.

Nadia Boulanger, who taught so many of us in Paris, is dead at 92, after a long coma. So the great influences of my life (in music) are now gone: Robert Casadesus and Nadia, and in a real way, Jacques Maritain and Arthur Lourie – all of whom were dear friends.

November 3, 1979

Dear Tom,

Your visit meant everything to me. After you left, I went back to bed and slept until 1:00 p.m. Last night I was violently ill, but when I did sleep, without sleeping pill or drugs, I slept the clock around.

John

November 5, 1979 (John's journal)

Fr. Tom came to be with us from Saturday until Friday of last week – a great blessing. He worked on some of his talks, slept a lot and resolved some of the problems of my unfinished works. He will edit the final years of Thomas Merton and the personal journals if I die or become totally disabled. That is a relief. He heard my confession and generally took care of me. There were times when I was very sick, but beyond that I felt a great happiness to have him here and I expect we both realized there is little chance I will see him again in this life.

November 8, 1979 (John's journal)

Another cold and dark day. The therapist came yesterday late in the evening and we did those leg, arm and stump exercises. I hurt so bad I could only sleep on my right side or sit up all during the night. Needed oxygen.

Friendship and Second Innocence

Tom called yesterday. Almost everyone at his office is ill – some kind of virus, so the work is piled up. I hope he does not catch it. He has important meetings this weekend.

It is almost 4:00 p.m. I have spent the day sitting in this wretched wheelchair, writing a few letters, trying to keep warm. I am trying to follow the drama in Iran, where over 60 Americans are held hostage unless we return the Shah (who is dying of cancer). We will not do that and the students are threatening to start killing the hostages and Khomeni is backing the students. God help us.

On the radio, we have the six Bach French suites played on the clavichord by Thurston Dart.

The doctor says I must take more food, more often. I have had broth again, with crackers, Instant Breakfast and now some grapefruit. What a mishmash, but it is all the system will tolerate.

The house is quiet. Piedy had to go to Dallas for a meeting of librarians today and will be there until late tonight. My mother is here babysitting me. Mandy, just home from school, is doing her homework. Now my mother is out picking up pecans – a very good crop this year – and I have to lie back down.

Later: after supper

Slept a while before supper, intending to listen to the news. Awakened for supper – creamed peas on toast, 1 egg, cheese & crackers, milk.

Too uncomfortable to sit up and type. I have to lie down again.

November 9, 1979

Dear Old Tommy,

Prof. Handa just called as I was coming out of a heart seizure. He said you and Rosanne had stopped by there on your way to Sharon. I am too weak to be sitting up, but I had the enclosed to send you – letter from Père Benedict, my reply, my notes for the day.

Professor Madan Handa at Regina Mundi Farm

Things are poor here. If you have nothing else planned for Christmas and if I am still able to tick, I have the money for a round-trip ticket for you. Please think it over, and if the time isn't already taken, keep it open to that possibility.

Love,

Johnny

November 9, 1979 (John's journal)

In bed until noon. The weather still so dark we need lights. It is supposed to turn cold this afternoon and tonight – our first real winter.

Yesterday, a department store called and offered my mother a credit card. Then they asked her what my father did. "Why, he's been dead almost four years," my mother said, after agreeing to take the card. The lady thanked her and hung up, refusing to give her the card. What a beastly injustice – not that it made that much difference to my mother, who usually pays cash for everything anyway. I am going to tell Piedy not to buy at that store anymore.

Benedict Vanier. Credit: John Howard Griffin.

Today is our son Johnny's 24th birthday. He sleeps almost all the time when he is home, because he works such killing hours on his job.

I am a zombie today. I type a line, wait a long time before another comes, try to pray, forget where I am. Am sedated, have severe phantom pains in the amputated leg and real pains in the other one, especially at the heel. The weather gets colder, darker. I feel like getting back into bed, but that seems to be a cop-out.

Later: Awakened from a deep sleep. Mail – very fine letters from Irv. Sussman, Joe Noonan, Fr. Benedict Vanier. Joe entered both himself (Bro. Infinitessimo) and me (Bro. Fervid) in the new volume of *Nobody: That's Who* – the kind of recognition all Maximinims of Milpitas deserve.

✶✶

3816 West Biddison
Fort Worth, TX 76109

November 9, 1979

Dear Father Benedict,

Thank you for your beautiful letter today. I am glad the book finally reached you all right. I think of you very often and thank God that our paths crossed; and I will never forget your kindness in bringing me the broth. Forgive the mistakes. My hands have little or no feeling now. I must soon go into the hospital again for further surgery and have very little heart function left. Fr. Tom McKillop came and spent a week with me recently – a great blessing.

God love you, dear friend. Thank you again for everything.

John Howard Griffin

1980

Friendship and Second Innocence

February 3, 1980 (John's journal)

Very sick. Much edema in the leg. Unable to sleep or to retain food. Even the stump has opened up again. How I long for sleep.

A kind of crisis occurred last night. From some dim memory came the phrase "God knows best" and then the answering question: "Is this really the best?" From some depth within me I made an act of faith, far more profound than those I have habitually made. I tried to read the Mass for today, but could not see the small print. I got up into my wheelchair, went into the bathroom and shaved ... at 2:00 a.m. Why, I don't know.

I returned to bed and tried to pray – for the sick; in thanksgiving for the good news that the Sussmans' book on Merton would now be published in paperback ... a tangle of prayers. Prayed for Fr. Beaudry, Sister Mary Ellen, for the soul of a young friend of my sons who committed suicide this week; for Fr. Tom and all his intentions; most of all for the strength to watch the doors close on my life without too much fear. I stay cold nearly all the time, and all the colour has gone from my hands.

What is to happen in the world? Long talk with Greg about this. Piedy wants him to leave the country rather than risk being drafted into another Vietnam situation. I told him we were with him whatever his decision. We are hearing, mostly in the over-50 age group, a positive lust for war. Greg remarked sardonically that was one way to get the population down.

May 17, 1980 (John's journal)

After a long silence, I have had them wheel the typewriter to the bed to make these notes. I have grown almost too weak to get even from the bed to the wheelchair without help. A nurse now comes twice a week to dress the wounds and take care of my needs – bathing, shaving, etc.

With very little vision left, I cannot enjoy reading any more. Fortunately, I pray without effort and for much of the time when I am awake. It is now something so natural that it is almost continuous. I have many books at the publishers, thanks to Tom McKillop's help – 22 volumes now, but have to do all the "business" by telephone, since I cannot usually find the strength to write letters.

Learned yesterday of the death of John Beecher at 76. He said he was looking forward to meeting Chaucer. I continue to get the most warming and wonderful letters from the Sussmans and Joe Noonan, thank God! Those, with frequent calls from Fr. Tom, keep me filled with gratitude.

A good note from Dan Berrigan, who is now back in New York, after a three-month stint in Berkeley.

May 18, 1980 (John's journal)

Awake at 8:00 a.m. Piedy had been up since 6:00, mowing the backyard. She brought coffee and we talked quite a while, mostly about black people we have known (and do know). Very pleasant. She had to help me get into my wheelchair this morning, though. I must get some strength some way. My stump and my leg are both quite swollen this morning.

May 19, 1980 (John's journal)

The legs swell more and more. The nurse was here this morning. She does not think the good leg can be saved, though it cannot be amputated because of the heart. I feel utterly miserable and sit up in the wheelchair to give my hips a rest from the constant lying in bed.

Insanity. A program tonight called "Jesus and the Superstars." That should be properly nauseating.

May 21, 1980 (John's journal)

A terrible spell, but I am some better today. Talked yesterday long distance with a friend who told me the reason we are holding the Maritain Symposium (dealing with the spirituality of Maritain and Merton) in Louisville at the Ramada Inn rather than at the Merton Center at Bellarmine is that the Merton Center people thought we were trying to use Merton's name to promote Maritain. This represents such an abysmal ignorance, I cannot believe it, especially in view of Merton's own written comment that he came to the faith through reading Maritain and Gilson.

"Poor Louie must be laughing," my informant said, speaking of Merton.

"More likely weeping," I said.

Later: Difficult days and nights. Much praying for Fr. Beaudry, who is apparently very near to or at the end of his life on earth.

Signed a contract with Andrews & McMeel this week for the hermitage diaries and have sent them photos to illustrate the book. So that is done. Thanks to Fr. Tom's editing. All of the volumes of journals except this one have now gone to the publishers – the two volumes to Andrews & McMeel, the other 20 to Houghton Mifflin.

May 25, 1980 – Pentecost (John's journal)

Quiet, very hot day, but cool in here with the air conditioners going. Piedy is washing. She got up early and mowed part of the lawn, but it was too hot to continue. Am propped up in the wheelchair while Piedy washes the bedclothes.

May 29, 1980 (John's journal)

Vernon Jordan, whom I used to visit in Atlanta before he became head of the Urban League, was shot in an assassination attempt and is near death, according to the news flashes. I know no more details at the moment.

Remarkable piece in current *Way* by Cornelia Sussman, on the marriage of Chanterelle and Shantidas. We were supposed to meet in Montreal in 1975, shortly after Chanterelle's death, but both Shantidas and I were ill and cancelled our meeting.

✶ ✶

May 31, 1980 (John's journal)

On a new antibiotic. The leg seems somewhat better, so I may have escaped the hospital this time.

Vernon Jordan is apparently going to live, thank God! He is still in very serious condition, but is no longer on the critical list. No solution yet as to who did it. He was shot twice in the back. The attempt occurred in Fort Wayne, Indiana.

June 1, 1980 (John's journal)

Awakened in the predawn hours by thunder and lightning. Moment of wonderful security here in my bed with the storm outside. I tried to stay awake to appreciate it but drifted quickly back into sleep.

Luiz de Moura Castro came last night with some friends. Brought a delicious shrimp and rice ring with mayonnaise, which they put together here. I did not visit much with them – slept much of the time while they visited Piedy in the den.

August 8, 1980 – Feast of St. Dominic (John's journal)

It is not in the results, but in the value, the rightness, the truth of the work itself. I am sure the rest takes care of itself in direct ratio as this orientation becomes our way of thinking and being.

This is why I long since remained aloof to "causes," organizations, slogans and myths … in themselves, when they had started as works dedicated to Jesus, or any Good, and then degenerated into themselves. But I have always cooperated with them whenever I could help.

At the end of my life, there are two words that express meaning for me now – Love and Innocence.

1980

Tommy McKillop: the last photo taken by John Howard Griffin

Last photo taken of John Howard Griffin.
Credit: Tom McKillop

Funeral Mass of John Howard Griffin

John Howard Griffin died on September 9, 1980. Three years before, as he was going back over his spiritual roots, he discovered an old missal that contained the scriptural readings read on the day of his birth, June 16, 1920. At the age of 57 he read them and was amazed at their seemingly prophetic message in relationship to the experience of his life.

Those same readings were proclaimed at his funeral on Thursday, September 11, 1980, at St. Andrew's Church in Fort Worth, Texas.—*Fr. Tom McKillop*

>You must not be surprised, brothers, when the world hates you; we have passed out of death and into life and of this we can be sure because we love our brothers. If you refuse to love, you must remain dead; to hate your brother is to be a murderer and murderers, as you know, do not have eternal life in them. This has taught us love – that He gave up His life for us; and we, too, ought to give up our lives for our brothers. If a man who was rich enough in this world's goods saw that one of his brothers was in need, but closed his heart to him, how could the love of God be living in him? My children, our love is not to be just words or mere talk, but something real and active.
>
>(John 3:13-18 – read by Fr. Tarcy)

I love you, Yahweh, my strength
(my saviour, you rescue me from violence),
Yahweh is my rock and my bastion, my deliverer is my God.

I take shelter in him, my rock,
my shield, my horn of salvation, my stronghold and my refuge.
From violence you rescue me.
He is to be praised; on Yahweh I call and am saved from my enemies.

The waves of death encircled me,
the torrents of Belial burst upon me,
the cords of Sheol girdled me, the snares of death were before me.
In my distress I called to Yahweh and to my God I cried;
from his Temple he heard my voice, my cry came to his ears.

(Psalm 18:1-6 – read by Mrs. Berber)

But he said to him, "There was a man who gave a great banquet, and he invited a large number of people. When the time for the banquet came, he sent his servant to say to those who had been invited 'Come along, everything is ready now.' But all alike started to make excuses. The first said, 'I have bought a piece of land and must go and see it. Please accept my apologies.' Another said, 'I have bought five yoke of oxen and am on my way to try them out. Please accept my apologies.' Yet another said, 'I have just got married and so am unable to come.'

The servant returned and reported this to his master. Then the householder, in a rage, said to his servant, 'Go out quickly into the streets and alleys of the town and bring in here the poor, the crippled, the blind and the lame.' 'Sir,' said the servant, 'your orders have been carried out and there is still room.' Then the master said to his servant, 'Go to the open roads and the hedgerows and force people to come in to make sure my house is full; because, I tell you, not one of those who were invited shall have a taste of my banquet.'"

(Luke 14:16-24 – read by Fr. Thompson)

Homily
by Fr. Tom McKillop

About a year ago, John Howard sent me a tape of these particular readings. He also sent me a number of letters. When I came down to see him at that time, because he was very sick, he spoke about death and about how, through life, he had chosen the readings for today. He had made reflections on them, I took some notes from what he had written and together what you are going to hear today is the truth of that reflection. So as you listen to what John Howard said, if anything seems to praise him, you'll know that it is not him who is saying it, but that it is a reflection of my own. As you listen to the words, think of it in relationship to the message that he wanted to share with you. At the end of the homily, there is a special song that he loved, which Paula Kriwoy and David Graham will come to the microphone and sing, to gather together what has been heard and hear out the message of that song.

Friendship and Second Innocence

John Howard believed that the way to peace among people was through authentic dialogue, whereby one did not treat the other as intrinsically other because of the differences of race, colour or creed, but tried to understand and overcome the obstacles to authentic communication to be able to receive and be received by the other to achieve peace.

There's a favorite passage of his that he chose from the journal of Raissa Maritain, the wife of Jacques Maritain, a very beloved friend. This is what she wrote, and this is what he felt summarized what he wanted to say.

> Men do not really communicate with each other except through the medium of being or one of its properties. If someone touches the true, like St. Thomas Aquinas, the contact is made. If someone touches the beautiful, like Beethoven, like Bloy or Dostoyevsky, the contact is made. If someone touches the good and love, like the Saints, the contact is made and souls communicate with each other.

One exposes oneself to not being understood when one expresses oneself without first having touched these depths. If one were to apply these words to the life of John Howard, with different names which he chose himself, this is what one might hear:

> If someone touches the true, like Jacques Maritain; if someone touches the beautiful, like Beethoven, Bach, Mozart, Monteverdi, Kurelek; if someone touches the good and Love, like Fr. Gerald Vann, Fr. Dominique Pire, Fr. Thomas Merton, Fr. Stan Murphy, then contact is made.

We all know that John reached these depths in communication. And the key for John Howard, in relationship to every person, was in going through what was true or beautiful till you came to the humanity of that person.

The word that he put in quotation marks was this: when he made contact with a person, he described that person as "pure gold."

I sent him a tape from Toronto that was a collection of taped messages that had been coming over a Toronto telephone from a radical right-wing group. He wanted to know what they were. When he sent the tape back, he had put the readings of his birth date with his reflections on it. This is what he said on the tape: "I can't bear anything with hate on it. I'm sending a message of human love, to wipe out the hate symbolically. If only we could wipe it out in people's hearts."

Fr. Tarcy read the first reading from the letter of John. These are the words that struck John Howard: "You must not be surprised, brothers, when the world hates you ... This has taught us love: that He gave up His life for us; and we, too, ought to give up our lives for our brothers ... Our love is not to be just words or mere talk, but something real and active."

And then he said these simple words because he was looking back 57 years at the words that were spoken the day of his birth. He was looking at it at the present time and saying this: "They're almost staggering. Dear Lord, isn't that extraordinary!"

When he read the psalm these are the words that came through to him. "In my distress I called to Yahweh and to my God I cried"; and then, from a different psalm, "Yahweh, you yourself are my lamp, my God lights up my darkness."

And when he reflected on the gospel that Fr. Thompson read, what he felt was that he had been called and that he had responded at one particular moment in what he described as being the great "yes." This was his total surrender. One way of expressing it concretely was a very personal and private way with regard to the vows he took with the Carmelites, which he did not speak about – vows of poverty and obedience. One thing he said at that time, he said right through the whole of his life, whatever he did: "I could never have done it without the help of my family."

His experience down through life, especially when he was going into the alleys of the world, sometimes made him feel that he was being patted on the back, but sometimes people rarely stayed beside you.

Through his life, his concerns with the blind, with racism, with young people, and in his latter days with the aged, as he went into the alleys of the world, one phrase stayed with him: "Jesus is in my heart."

During the last couple of years, two persons meant a great deal to him: Dr. Viktor Frankl and Don Helder Camara, Archbishop of Recife, Brazil. Dr. Frankl spoke of how you join the humane minorities rather than drift as part of the voiceless majorities. Don Helder Camara said we have to become part of the Abrahamic minorities – people who will be willing to go out into the unknown not knowing where they are going, close to the Cross. These were a central conviction for John Howard.

The tape contained these eight lines. These were lines from his favourite gospel, from the feast of Our Lady of Mt. Carmel. If we listen to them again, we hear how profoundly they incarnated the very flesh of John Howard Griffin.

> Jesus knew this and withdrew from the district. Many followed Him and He cured them all, but He warned them not to make Him known. This was to fulfill the prophecy of Isaiah: Here is my servant whom I have chosen, my beloved, the favorite of my soul. I will endow him with my spirit and he will proclaim the true faith to the nations. He will not brawl or shout ... nor will any hear his voice in the streets. He will not break the crushed reed, nor put out the smouldering wick till he has led the truth to victory: in his name the nations will put their hope. (Matthew 12:15-21)

The favourite patron saint of John Howard – and he probably had many of them, but one stayed with him – was John the Baptist. Just about eight or nine days ago was the feast of the death of John the Baptist. The very essential letter of John the Baptist's life was in speaking about Jesus: "He must increase, I must decrease."

In John Howard's very private and very personal life and spiritual life, the way he described the Indwelling Person was the "Beloved." His favourite prayer was the Jesus prayer – "Jesus, Son the living God, have mercy on me a sinner" – and the question he asked himself throughout his life was this: "Can one man simply do the will of God as directed under obedience – not my will, but His?"

There is a favorite passage from Thomas Merton, which John sent on the feast of St. Dominic, on August 8, 1977. He sent it to me personally, but he thought of this when he spoke of today. So many of us who are concerned with making a better world are often caught up in the necessary meaning of results and how much we look for success. John not only edited Thomas Merton's letter, he also put his comment at the end of it. This is what he wrote: "This is Thomas Merton speaking to you and me. He wrote this to a young man in social justice."

> The next step is for you to see that your own thinking about what you are doing is crucially important. You are probably striving to build yourself an identity in your work, out of your work and your witness. You are using it, so to speak, to protect yourself against nothingness, annihilation. That is not the right use of your work. All the good that you will do will come not from you, but from the fact that you have allowed yourself, in the obedience of faith, to be used by God's love. Think of this more and gradually you will be free from the need to prove yourself and you can be more open to the power that will work through you without your knowing it. The great thing after all is to love, not to pour out your life in the service of a myth; and we turn the best things into myths.
>
> If you can get free from the domination of causes and just serve Christ's truth, you will be able to do more and will be less crushed

> by the inevitable disappointments. Because I see nothing whatever in sight but disappointment, frustration and confusion ... The real hope then, is not something we think we can do, but in God who is making something good out of it in some way we cannot see. If we can do His will, we will be helping in the process. But we will not necessarily know all about it beforehand ...
>
> Also, "the big results are not in your hands or mine, but they suddenly happen and we can share in them; but there is no point in building our lives on this personal satisfaction, which may be denied us and which after all is not that important....

That was written on February 21, 1966. John Howard commented on that text. This is what he said:

> Certainly, that advice conforms to my own experience. I believe it is a terribly important key and clue to everyone involved in any kind of working for the good of mankind. It is almost the only viewpoint that can allow us to persevere in what otherwise appears to be thankless and totally ungratifying activity. It is not in the results, but in the value, the rightness, the truth of the work itself.
>
> I am sure the rest takes care of itself in direct ratio as this orientation becomes our way of thinking and being. This is why I long since remained aloof to "causes," organizations, slogans and myths ... in themselves, when they had started works dedicated to Jesus, or any Good and then degenerated into themselves; although I have always co-operated with them whenever I could help.

John, in his relationship to love, said this simple but profound thought: "Each of us begins as a child, innocent; each of us as an adult must come to a second innocence, where you know and experience evil and you choose to be childlike." What a profound thought for a life of acceptance.

Funeral Mass of John Howard Griffin

Last week when I was in the hospital room with John, Fr. Judge, the pastor of the parish, came. John was very sick and very weak, extremely fragile. Fr. Judge asked him if he would like to receive Holy Communion. John wasn't able to swallow anything. Father gave him a small portion of the Host, then he took a plastic cup of water and he held it six inches from his mouth. It seemed to take too long for him to be able to sip a portion of water. When he did, he looked down and he prayed for a short while and with all the pain that he was feeling he said to Fr. Judge, "Father, would you like a cup of coffee?" To me, that was John Howard Griffin!

Shortly afterwards, when the priest had left John felt very fragile. He said, "It's so hard to be reduced to nothing! All I have left now is the pure silence of love."

There is one great saying that John used in his talks in the '60s. It is a phrase from Edmund Burke. Wherever John went, he seemed to send this message out because it meant so much to him. "All that is necessary for the triumph of evil is that good men do nothing."

Two years ago, when he was very ill, he thought over those words. He wanted to say something positive, something that would be a real truth, something encouraging. These are the words that he came to, near the end of his life:

> All that is necessary to triumph over evil is that good men and women with integrity, living in the Beloved, do good over and over, again and again, together.

Afterword

Deacon Frank McLean, a Permanent Deacon at St. John Chrysostom Parish in Newmarket, Ontario, listened to me one day as I reflected on friendship and second innocence. He felt that there needed to be a follow-up to the dialogue. I let the thought reach my heart and wondered about the possibilities.

Later I reflected on the future coming towards us and dreamed these words as the new century was beginning:

> The 21st Century is coming towards us
> With possibilities, challenges and decisions. The
> 20th Century has brought to us Experiences of
> profound individualism, Competition, isolation
> and independence. At the close of the Century
> There are hopeful signs
> Of coming together in communion
> Microcosms of interdependence
> The future is bringing to us
> A dream for Friendship and Second Innocence.
> Based on the Gospel of St. Matthew Jesus says
> prophetically
> "Again, truly I tell you,
> If two of you agree on earth
> About anything you ask,
> It will be done by my Father in heaven,
> For where two or three are gathered In my name,
> I am there among them." (Matthew 18:19-20)

Fr. Tom McKillop
St. John Chrysostom Parish

On the Trail of a Photograph

The following is an e-mail sent to Robert Bonazzi, executor of the John Howard Griffin Estate, by photographer Bill Wittman. The letter outlines the path of recovering an important photograph that appears on page 124 of this book.

January 16, 2008

Hi, Robert:

When this all started, all we had was Fr. Tom's photocopy of a photograph showing John sitting with a couple – Louis and Eunice Thompson – who had visited John in early July 1977.

John sent a letter to Tom on July 17, 1977, and included the photograph. This letter of John's discusses some of the central themes of his work. The original photograph is lost; Tom strongly wished the photocopy to be included, but the publisher felt that it would not print well and decided to omit it. I agreed with this assessment.

On hearing and accepting this decision, Fr. Tom requested that I help him find another print of the photograph. I agreed to start the hunt. I must acknowledge that I was only doing it for Tom – to humour him, to show my commitment – and as a follow-through to John's directive to me so many years ago to "take care of Tommy." I did not believe it would be possible to find the photo. It was 30 years ago, and it was just a family snapshot. I didn't expect there would be more than one copy in existence. Impossible!

My first few attempts confirmed this belief. I couldn't even find an easy way of contacting you. I told Tom things were not looking good. He was accepting, but remained hopeful and encouraging. I continued the search, but I was sure I was on a fool's errand.

Then came the beginning of a breakthrough. I was able to connect with you, and you were encouraging. While you did not have knowledge of the photo, or hope of accessing it from John's negatives, you had an ongoing relationship with the Thompsons' son, Fr. August Thompson. This was amazing! A miracle! I knew Fr. August was mentioned in John's correspondence. He might have a memory of the visit, and maybe even a picture. Your ability to enable this connection was a transforming moment. Finding some reference to a photo was now a faint possibility. I knew Tom would be thrilled.

The next step had mixed results. When I corresponded with Fr. August by e-mail, using your name as a reference, he recalled the visit and thought he might have a photo taken that day. But he didn't believe there was any chance of his finding it.

I went back to Tom with this problem. Tom was quick to suggest the obvious: see if Fr. August had any photo of his parents that could be used as a substitute.

I e-mailed Fr. August with this suggestion, along with more encouragement to look for the desired photo, saying, "Perhaps an inspiration may come as to the photo's whereabouts, and it will gently call your name."

A couple of days later Fr. August wrote back. He had found his photograph of the visit with John and his parents, as well as a photo of his parents celebrating their 50th wedding anniversary! He was sending both photographs to me by post.

So, an essential photo has been recovered. This photograph is not exactly the same as the one John sent to Fr. Tom back in 1977. It was probably taken two seconds before or after. But it is an even richer image than Tom's photocopy. In addition to the Thompson couple and John, it also includes Fr. August and Elizabeth.

Thanks to you for your central role in this wondrous story.

Bill Wittman

Recognition

Listed in the manuscript of letters and fragments are the names of these persons, who knowingly or unknowingly, entered into the inclusive friendship, dialogue and graced communion of John Howard Griffin and Tom McKillop.

Sr. Mary Alban; Albert & Karen; Marion Anderson; Andrews & McMeel; Bailey, at the Skyline; Fr. Beaudry; Dan Berrigan; Leon Bloy; Bonnie, at Maplehurst; Phyllis Bowman; Fr. Brière; Ivan Burgess; Don Burton; Archbishop Helder Camara of Recife, Brazil; Robert Casedesus; Chanterelle & Shantidas; Cesar Chavez; Group Captain Leonard Cheshire; Fr. Clayton; Jim Corrigal; Gordon Cressey; Fr. George Curtsinger; Sr. Marguerite Davies; Dorothy Day; Luiz & Bridget De Moura Castro; Catherine Doherty; James & Shelley Douglass; Father Dan Egan; John Mary Eudes; Sr. Flynn; Dr. Ford; Dr. Viktor Frankl; Bishop Thomas Fulton; Fr. Terry Gallagher; Maxwell & Peter Geismar; Chief Dan George; David Graham; Dick Gregory; Elizabeth (Piedy) Griffin; Susan, John, Gregory and Mandy Griffin; John Girard; Professor Madan Handa; Roland Hayes; Father Augustine Healy; Clyde Holland; Jean Hussar; Penn Jones; Vernon Jordan; Linda Kay: Clyde Kennard; Martin Luther King; Chris Knowles; Paula Kriwoy; Elisabeth Kübler-Ross; Hans Küng; Dr. Kyger; Msgr. Lacey; Claudette Le Blanc; George Levitan; Louis Liege; Arthur Lourie; Frank Lynch; Marco; Jacques Maritain; Raissa Maritain; Markoe Brothers; Maximinims of Milpitas; Alf McCabe; Ellen McCormack; Gerry & Kitty McGilly; Mrs. Mary McKillop; Fr. Thomas Merton; Malcolm Muggeridge; John Murphy; Joe Noonan; Fr. Henri Nouwen; Bill O'Donnell; Fr. Jim O'Donnell; Deba Patknik; Brother Patrick; Fr. Philip; Fr. Dominique Pire; Henriette Pierre; Bob Quayle; Abraham Rattner; Ruth Reverdy; Bambi Rutledge; Sr. St. Raymond; Mary Sallison; Silvano Salvaterra; Simon Scanlon;

Sr. Gwen Smith; Tom Snyder; Fr. Stan; Rudy Stocking; Cornelia Sussman; Fr. Tarcy; Mother Teresa; Fr. Thompson & parents; Studs Turkel; John Turner; Benedict Vanier; Jean Vanier; Vera; Tony Walsh; Paul Woodcroft.

Youth Corps

Roots

The scriptural foundation of Youth Corps is found in Chapters 9 and 10 of the Gospel of Luke.

Mission Statement

Youth Corps strives to co-create communities of Christian leaders, especially among the youth, rooted in their liberating faith in Jesus Christ, through:

ACTION, REFLECTION AND FRIENDSHIP

With others, we seek to overcome the forces militating against life, through the development of authentic relationships, critical awareness and a church of justice and love.

We tend to work in small teams, the working together of young and adult, moving to be centred in Jesus.

Original events and later development

The year was 1967. Dr. Timothy O'Leary was promoting to young people the escapism of drugs and chemicals as a positive experience. The media gave him massive coverage.

To offset such people as Dr. O'Leary, Youth Corps gathered together in 1966 a number of people to dream what we could do to bring people to the city who were living a truth with a dynamic faith. We hoped to inspire young people with realness rather than watch them be seduced by unrealness. We booked Convocation Hall at the University of Toronto (where O'Leary had been scheduled to appear), called it "The Event," and because it was Canada's centennial year, asked a Canadian, Dr. Jean Vanier, the founder of L'Arche communities, to be our first speaker.

Over the years, other Event speakers were those whose approach to social issues demands a response from all people of good will. Event presenters included John Howard Griffin, Dorothy Day, Fr. Dan Egan, Mother Teresa, Leonard Cheshire, Viktor Frankl, Elizabeth Kübler-Ross, Chief Dan George, Jim Wallis, Dom Helder Camara, Frank Sheed and Catherine Doherty.

We believed that the young and the young-in-spirit should be given the opportunity to hear, study, and know these great witnesses and role models.

Eventually, the event moved to Massey Hall. Mother Teresa spoke at three different events. Each time, the crowd grew larger. The last event with her was held at Varsity Stadium, where she addressed no fewer than 20,000 people.

The Sharon Corps Vision

As a community centred on the vision of Jesus we seek to grow in love, forgiveness and justice, learning this through service and action to enable others to hear the same call.

We seek to create an atmosphere that can captivate and touch people's hearts so that this challenge will grow on and beyond the Christian Family Peace Weekends.

The Sharon Corps Community, 1972–1997

Youth Corps Team Members 1966–1999*

Fr. Tom McKillop; Sr. Noreen Allossery, osu; Sr. Judy Atherton, csj; Elizabeth Barreca; Laurie Bell; Marnie Bell; Gina Blair; Art Blomme; Fr. Terry Bolland, ofm, cap.; Steve Bransfield; Bob Carty; Leslie Charbon; Ross Coiterman; Patsy Coulter; Dale Crocock; Trevor Digby; Fr. Eduardo Do Couto; Tia Durkin; Denise Fleming; Sr. Mary Flynn, csj; Lorraine Fontaine-O'Connell; Denise Fox; Fr. Terry Gallagher sfm; Daniel Gana; Dave Graham; Gina Grimaldi; Dave Hasbury; Teresa Healy; Trevor Hilton; Karen Hinds; Bob Interbartolo; Joe James; Elly Kaas; Sr. Maureen Killoran, cnd; Paula Kriwoy; Don Lizzotti Leonard; Sarah Macdougall; Bob McCabe; Mike McDonough; Paul McDonough; Gerry McGilly; Melissa Meeker; Bernie Merrett; Joe Mihevc; Lola Murphy; Fernand Oliveira; Sr. Margaret Ordway, IBVM; Pam O'Shea; Rosanne Pellizzari; Fr. Charlie Pottie, sj; Louisa Quarta; Kelly Rico; Sharon Robinson; Karen Ruttiman; Silvano Salvaterra; Nancy Segmeister; Les Smith; Sr. Gwen Smith, csj; Joseph So; Bambi Stokes; Dwyer Sullivan; Terry Sullivan; Jodie Warner; Elizabeth Willenbrook; Fr. Paul Woodcroft; Simon Yuen

Team Secretaries: Marnie Bell; Arlene Carruthers; Aggie Cekuta; Anne Medeiros-Oliveira; Annemarie Petrasek; Sylvia Petrasek; Rosemarie White

* These are the most complete lists we could provide.

An argument arose among them as to which one of them was the greatest. But Jesus, aware of their inner thoughts, took a little child and put it by his side, and said to them, "Whoever welcomes this child in my name welcomes me, and whoever welcomes me welcomes the one who sent me; for the least among all of you is the greatest." (Luke 9:46-48)

> Youth Corps is a Child.
> Jesus is the child.

"For where two or three are gathered in my name, I am there among them." (Matthew 18:20)

Tommy McKillop receives the Order of Canada, June 29, 2005
(L-R: Fr. Terry Gallagher, S.F.M., Governor General Michaëlle Jean, Tommy McKillop, Susan Rosgen, Collette Skelly)

This book has been printed on 100% post consumer waste paper, certified Eco-logo and processed chlorine free.